LATE LIFE ADVENTURES IN LONDON AND BEYOND

Late Life Adventures

Book 1

ANNEMARIE RAWSON

*'Go confidently in the direction of your dreams.
Live the life you have imagined.'*
Henry David Thoreau

Contents

Prologue

It's never too late to follow your dreams and live the life you have imagined ... hold that thought.

February 2018, I was surrounded by open cartons, every surface covered in kitchen paraphernalia, waiting to be packed and shipped off for long-term storage. The house was a bomb site. It was a *déjà vu* moment, so reminiscent of our move to France, and feeling just as chaotic.

Steve's job ended during a round of redundancies announced in August 2017. He'd stay on until December but then what? He was 61. It was going to be an uphill battle trying to secure a comparative job and income at that age. Male, stale and pale – in the eyes of many employers.

"I'm tired of social norms and expectations dictating how we should live, Steve. Do the classic '9 to 5 job, seven days a week until you retire at 65' thing." Sitting on the sofa, fuming, my head was whirling with 'what-should-we-do-now?' questions. I twirled my empty wine glass in my hand, contemplating whether to refill it, and turned to look at him.

"Sod it!" I banged the glass down on the table. "You've got a

British passport. Why don't we just pack up and move to London? See what happens? Or do what Malc suggested?"

"Hang on a minute. That's a bit drastic. Let's just see if I can get a job here first," Steve countered, hunched over his laptop trawling through jobs listed on Seek. He wasn't one to decide hastily and needed time to digest new ideas – such as moving 12,000 miles across the world (again), with no job prospects in sight. Fair enough.

I was incredibly frustrated. *You* might have a life plan, but businesses could retrench at any time, smashing *your* plan to smithereens. I was still working on the front desk at Nigel Parr, an oral surgeon in Auckland, but I was starting to feel past it with such a young, front-of-house crew now on board. It was time for me to move on.

I got to my feet, opened the fridge door and, reaching for the nearly empty wine bottle, tossed a few more words over my shoulder. "Well, I'm not going to wait for anyone else to say yes, a job's yours, or no it's not. I've had enough of others having control over our lives. C'mon. Steve. Our place can be rented out and we can use that income to pay rent and feed ourselves somewhere in London while we look for work. And if we must dig into our retirement savings, well so be it." I poured the dregs of the bottle into my wine glass, kicking the fridge door shut behind me.

Do I sound belligerent? I was at the time, feeling so fed up. I just got a grunt and a swift glance before Steve continued his search.

I pushed on, exploring my idea of possibly packing up and moving overseas again. We'd done it before, taking estate manager roles in Southwest France and, apart from a few rough months, it had been the best time of our lives. I wrote our story in the books *My French Platter* and *My French Platter Replenished*. With nothing to lose and fabulous life experiences to gain, why not give London a go too?

During our visit to France in 2017, Malc, a friend of ours with the London Fire Brigade, suggested to Steve he retrain as a fire risk assessor. Malc put Steve in touch with an ex-colleague, Alan, who owned a fire risk assessment business in the UK. After some research, there looked to be plenty of this work available in London. Steve followed up the contact and once he'd come round to the idea of living in London and our flights were sorted, he booked into the appropriate Fire Protection Association course, starting three weeks after we arrived. Alan then suggested Steve contact him again once we were settled.

Friends Ken and Irene, who lived in York, owned a flat in London but I'd no idea where, or how often they used it. Now that my plan of upping sticks and moving to London was taking shape, I sent them a message asking if they still owned it and whether it might be available for us to rent.

"You must be psychic, Annemarie," Ken replied. "The grandkids and family are moving to Edinburgh, so we'll have no need to go to London any longer. I just said to Irene let's put the flat on the rental market. It's yours if you want it. It's in Teddington, down beside the Thames. I think you'd like it there and it would be brilliant knowing you were looking after the place. I'll send you photos."

I started this memoir in a huge mess but now, with everything packed and finalised, and at the age of 60, we were on the verge of another exciting adventure. I couldn't wait to begin. Would we last six months? Would we stay for five years? Time would tell ...

MARCH 2018
TEDDINGTON; RICHMOND;
PETERSHAM NURSERIES; BUSHY PARK;
HAM HOUSE; HAMPTON COURT
PALACE

We blew into Heathrow on 2 March 2018 with four suitcases and the Beast from the East – a wild storm of blizzards, drifting snow and bitter cold, causing death and destruction throughout the UK. It was the worst weather they'd had in years. The forty-hour journey, door-to-door, was uneventful but tiring and we were so grateful to find Ken waiting for us in Arrivals.

Our new home in Teddington was only a twenty-minute drive from Heathrow, but the car wipers were flying furiously trying to keep up with the sleet slashing the windscreen. During a brief respite, Steve and Ken hauled our luggage up to the flat. I clambered up two flights of stairs ahead of them, my cabin bag banging against my leg, to find Irene standing in the doorway, her arms opened wide. She engulfed me in a big hug, as did a whoosh of comforting heat escaping through the open door.

"Welcome you two! You must be exhausted from that long trip and freezing after your hot New Zealand summer. The heating's on. C'mon. Give us your coats." Irene bustled us through the door, stripping the coats off our backs as we went, indicating the bathroom to the right, our bedroom on the left, turning us down the hallway and passing the kitchen on the way to the sitting room.

It may have been snowing outside, but plenty of light still streamed through the large picture windows at each end of the sitting room. I was immediately drawn to the one that looked out over the park next door. The grass was now a white-flecked carpet. Huge stark-naked, horse chestnut trees ran in a short avenue towards the river, where a tarmac terrace with snow-covered bench seats ran along the front, overlooking the Thames and across to Teddington Lock. The opposite window had a more utilitarian view of a slushy driveway, garages and car park, and the steps to the front door of the block of flats.

"Right, cup of tea first." Ken was rubbing his hands together, trying to get some feeling back in his fingers. "Then you can tell us all the news and what your plans are while we have lunch. I'll put the kettle on."

A delicious aroma wafted through from the kitchen. Irene had prepared pulled pork and coleslaw to have with buns so, sitting at the dining table, sinking our teeth into the scrumptious food, we swapped family news and heard who else lived in the flats.

Several hours later and failing to stifle a yawn, I apologised to Ken and Irene. "Sorry I look such a wreck. It's the jet lag, lack of sleep, lovely food – and no make-up." I was starting to wilt in the warmth and ran my fingers through my hair, trying to push it into some sort of order.

"Don't worry, Annemarie, you're fine. You've spent 40 hours getting here," Irene placated. Standing and stacking our empty plates, she suggested, "Once we've shown you the ropes of how the flat works and where everything is, I think we should all go out. I know it's still snowing lightly but it'll help keep you awake. Let's get the bus to Kingston-Upon-Thames, have a quick look around there, then walk our High Street when we get back."

Kingston had a great shopping precinct with everything we could possibly need. Aldi, Waitrose, Sainsbury's and M&S were all in easy reach of each other too. The elegant Bentall Centre and cobbled streets seemed to be filled with every chain store in the UK as well as smart, independent boutiques. My head was swivelling, trying to take in all the gorgeous homeware, clothes, shoes and boots in the window displays. Everything was so different from that on offer in New Zealand. I couldn't wait to come back and spend an afternoon wandering through all these stores.

We discovered that Kingston-Upon-Thames played a vital part in early English royal history. An ancient stone block, known as the coronation stone, is believed to be where seven Anglo-Saxon kings were crowned, dating from the year 925. The stone is protected by heavy wrought-iron railings.

Teddington was just perfect too, with a busy High Street full of cafés, restaurants, enticing pubs and boutiques. I was looking forward to seeing it all without the snow and sleet, which turned our eyes to slits and finally drove us back to the shelter and warmth of the flat and more cups of tea.

"Right, we'll leave you to it. We're staying at our friend's place near Esher for the night. If you need anything in a hurry, just give us a yell. You've got our numbers," Ken said an hour later, hauling a reluctant Irene up off the sofa. She wasn't looking forward to facing the elements after being snug and warm in the flat. It was now late afternoon and darkness had descended. They gathered up their bits and bobs, hugged us goodbye and Steve and I saw them to the door.

"Thanks so much for everything. We're thrilled to be here. I can't believe how it all worked out and I can't wait to go exploring – once this snow stops of course," I yawned noisily and waved them off down the stairs.

"Right, let's get unpacked now before we hit the wall and start dribbling from jet lag." Steve was keen to get sorted and pushed our wheeled cases into the bedroom.

"Now?" I wailed, gawping at him. It was the last thing I wanted to do. But I knew if I sat down again, I'd fall asleep. The wardrobe was a double, with floor-to-ceiling sliding mirrored doors, and it looked spacious.

"Yes, now. C'mon. Won't take long." Steve stood with hands on hips, nodding at the wardrobe. "I'm sure you'll easily fill this with all your stuff. I don't mean with just what's in these suitcases, but when our cartons arrive. I'll use the two big cupboards in the hallway. One has a rail and there are plenty of shelves in the second. That'll work." Steve unzipped his first case and got started.

I was glad we did it, once everything was finally put away. Our summer clothing and shoes, plus hiking boots and poles and Steve's work boots, had been sent by sea, leaving us to bring our warmer gear in the suitcases.

My head was feeling very woolly, but before I fell into bed, I wanted to inspect the kitchen properly. It was compact but modern and contained everything we needed, including a food processor, rice cooker and a wok. Everything was good quality and would be perfect for us. Irene had been so kind and got in the basics for us, plus she'd left all their herbs and spices and tinned food, as well as bits in the freezer. We'd leave it the same, when it came time for us to return to New Zealand.

The living area was spacious, with a six-seater dining table and full bookcase at the car park end. Two large sofas, a coffee table, a large display/storage cabinet and TV unit with a huge TV and stereo system were at the park end. The picture windows really made the flat special.

"Aren't we lucky, Steve. Getting this flat," I said to him, yawning my head off. We'd had another pulled pork bun for dinner and a cup of tea and we were both fading fast.

"We absolutely are. It's perfect and all we need," he agreed. "C'mon. Let's get to bed. Hopefully the weather will be better in the morning, and we can get out exploring."

"Be there in a minute." I took one last look around the sitting room, still not really believing we'd arrived, before switching off the lights and heading for the bathroom. I was shattered but full of anticipation of what was ahead of us and I couldn't wait to start 'living' our London life.

We'd hardly caught our breath when, two days later, bundled up in coats, scarves and gloves, we caught the train into Waterloo to meet up with friends, Richard and Bridget at The Ivy Market Grill, a fabulous little restaurant right in the heart of Covent Garden. They'd taken a train down from Northamptonshire to share Bridget's birthday celebration lunch with us.

Several hours passed in a blur enjoying good food, wine and conversation. With jet lag still very much in my system, as well as too much Picpoul de Pinet, my eyelids were drooping. It was time to head home.

That was the beginning. Our diaries began filling up with old friends in London, those due to visit and, of course, with our son, Murdoch who lived there. So many New Zealand friends too, were booked to come through London over the summer, on their way to European holidays and avoiding winter back home. There was so much to look forward to.

With this new life came lots of administration. First things first; UK cell phone numbers. A quick visit to Three and we were set up, with the Post Office providing our broadband. So many services hinged on providing a utility bill and our rental agreement, to prove where we lived. No one is ever thrilled to receive a bill, but we were, when that first power bill arrived.

Clutching this, our passports and rental agreement, we presented ourselves at the NatWest bank in Kingston and opened our UK account. Next to tick off was our National Health Insurance (NHI) numbers, which would give us access to the health system. Several phone calls and two days later, these too came through and enrolment forms had been completed and dropped off at the recommended doctor and dentist in the High Street. Progress.

Discovering new places with everything being 'new' to us was quite exhilarating. I couldn't wait for spring to arrive to see the trees in the park next door in full leaf and spend long, warm evenings in there. As time went on, I would often be drawn to the windows. There was always something happening. The park, through a gate on the perimeter, would become our garden where we'd take a glass of wine before dinner to sit and watch all the goings-on on the water, and we'd often return with a cup of tea afterwards.

"One week down and most of the admin sorted. Any regrets?" Steve asked, putting my cup of tea on the coffee table and dropping down beside me onto the couch.

"Even in my jet lag fug and feeling disorientated, absolutely none. I can't believe our luck, to be honest," I admitted. "Everything has fallen into place, and *we* have fallen on our feet with this flat."

Our location was brilliant. The flat was a short walk to Teddington Lock and Bridge which immediately led onto one of the many Thames Paths. These paths total 186 miles and connect so many parts of London and beyond. And what a bonus to discover that the centre of London (Waterloo station) was only 35 minutes by train.

The bus stops, taking us in all directions and to the tube in Richmond and Heathrow Airport, were literally around the corner. The High Street gave us all that we needed, too. The flat was brilliant, with plenty of storage and a dry garage as well.

We loved it and I pinched myself, thinking this was just the beginning of a voyage of discovery. Day trips were on my agenda, the first one being in mid-April to see the flush of bluebells in the gardens of Chartwell, Churchill's home in Kent.

During that first week though, I'd wangled an interview with a dentist in the High Street for a part-time receptionist role and one with a 'lady of importance' – to fly with her to her *manoir* in Normandy to assist with a week-long house party she was hosting in May. *Ooh la la!* She sounded delightful and wanted to make it a fun-filled experience for the person who got the job. I hoped she'd pick me.

During our second week we received our 60+ Oyster photo ID cards. These cards would transform our lives while living in London, both financially and in the sense that we could travel wherever we liked on all tube, bus and overground rail services free of charge within the 1–9 London zones. There had to be a catch, right? No, there wasn't. The only requirements were to be at least 60 years of age and to live in one of the London boroughs. However, our train line was the South Western which, unfortunately, was the only line that restricted the use of the card before 9.30 a.m. on weekdays. But we could work around that. The card would end up saving us thousands of pounds while we lived there.

The popular Anglers pub around the corner was only a hop, skip and a jump from our driveway. We planned on going to the quiz nights and hopefully join a table, to meet people. Everyone we met the first time we went in was friendly, including the two barmen, so we stopped to have a drink and a chat. The pub was cosy and homely, with a roaring fire burning in the grate. The beer garden at the rear was enormous, with about thirty tables, and the children's playground was apparently a huge draw in the summer. The property extended down to the water's edge of the Thames and included a jetty, so it was easy to imagine it filled with mums and dads relaxing and shrieking children charging around on a warm summer's day.

Two rooms were set off to the side of the bar itself where you could sit and read or play board games and do puzzles. A group in their early thirties were having a boisterous, fun competition to see who could complete a kid's jigsaw puzzle in the shortest time. It was entertaining, watching them grabbing pieces, each desperate to win. Books lined one wall and, for a small fee, patrons could borrow one. It was like being in someone's home; it was such a convivial and inviting place to be.

On one of our early forays, Steve and I left the house rugged up in our puffa jackets, beanies, scarves and gloves and ventured out to Twickenham, famous for its international rugby stadium. It was an easy twenty-minute walk from our driveway, and our heads swivelled left and right, checking out the lovely homes along the route with some on the right, running down to the water's edge.

Church Street in Twickenham is pedestrianised at weekends, blocked off at each end by large, wheeled boxes overflowing with colourful blooms and trailing ivy. The street is cobbled and lined both sides with beautiful little boutiques selling wines, craft beers, charcuterie, books and LP records, gifts, elegant clothing and homeware, and sitting in amongst the small Mediterranean restaurants and cafés is the most divine Italian deli and sweet shop.

"Wow, this place is fabulous, Steve. We'll come here again – so many different eateries. It'll be hard to choose. We'll wait until we've got work and then I'll book one of them."

"Definitely. But right now, I'm just going to check out the craft beers up here. I'll see you back in the street somewhere." Steve was off like a rocket, darting into the shop. I was sure he'd return with a package under his arm.

This was a busy and charming little street and we were both drooling walking through it – Steve was thinking of the food and beers and I of the clothing, shoes and homeware. The Eel Pie pub, named after the nearby Eel Pie Island, with a great gastro pub menu and no eel pie in sight, stands proudly at the end of the street. The island's name is thought to come from the inn on the island which served eel pies in the nineteenth century, because of the abundance of eels in the surrounding waters. The only access to the island then was via watercraft and it became a popular stopping point for steamer excursions.

A short distance from Church Street is the classically elegant York House, which has its formal gardens on the other side of the road, running along the back of Twickenham and adjacent to the Thames. These gardens are home to the most incredible, ornate marble fountain, set at one end of the landscaped garden, where life-sized female sculptures, mythical beasties and huge clam shells are set high up into the rocks and mosses. Water cascades down the clam shells at various levels and into the pond itself, where lily pads float on the filmy surface. Lawned areas hide behind trimmed hedges, and park benches are set out in sunny spots. Squirrels scurry everywhere and are so tame. We saw one take food from a man's hand.

York House itself is a former stately home with a wonderful history and its front and rear gardens are connected by an arched stone bridge built over the bisecting road. The arch itself is a feat of engineering and a work of beauty.

A few doors down is Dial House, with its fabulous sundial sitting high up on the façade. It bears the date 1726 and the name Thomas Twining – the famous tea merchant. This was the country house of the Twining family way back then and latterly, the home of Elizabeth Twining until her death in 1889. She bequeathed this beautifully crafted brick home to the local church and it became the vicarage.

Our first food shopping expeditions were eye-opening experiences, starting with the Kingston-Upon-Thames market, held in the elegant town square where a gilded statue of Queen Anne keeps watch, perched high above the parapet of Market Square House. I couldn't believe how affordable the vegetables were, even when we converted from British pounds to New Zealand dollars. The exchange rate meant everything we bought cost us double the price. A *whole* cauliflower was only £1 ($2), raspberries and blueberries were £1 a punnet, and sweet potato (known as kumara in New Zealand) was an astonishing £1.50 ($3.00) for a bag of six medium-sized ones.

Discovering the M&S £10 dinner-for-two meals was a little treat too. The £10 bought a choice of a main course, a salad and/or veg and a pudding – and a bottle of wine was thrown in too. We couldn't quite believe that and, if the wine wasn't that great, it could always be used for cooking. Funnily enough, our wine never did get used for cooking ... Waitrose often did the £10 meals too and was the only supermarket to sell our much-loved Vogel's bread – cheaper and denser than in New Zealand and tasting just as good.

However, Aldi became our supermarket of choice. No, it didn't have everything but certainly covered all the basics and we could top up at any one of the other stores with what Aldi couldn't supply. The prices in the London supermarkets brought home how ridiculously expensive our food was in New Zealand. I'm sure the size of the population had a lot to do with it, but New Zealand is an agricultural country, for heaven's sake. I just didn't understand it but knew we exported as much as possible, leaving us to pay a higher price for what was left.

After ten days living together in a one-bedroom flat in Teddington, Steve had had enough of my 10,000+ words a day and gave up being my best friend. He resorted to his headphones and pretended to study. I wasn't hurt – much (she says, tongue-in-cheek). Steve's workbooks for the Certificate in Applied Fire Risk Management course had arrived and he'd got stuck in. There was so much reading to get through to prepare for the course and the exam that followed, so I left him to it, happily taking myself out walking.

The weather was the dominating factor in our lives as we were totally reliant on 'Shanks' Pony' and public transport to get around. Before heading out each day, we'd be online checking the day's forecast and temperature. It felt as though spring wasn't far away. Pretty pink buds were about to burst open on the trees around us and, on the front lawn, sunny yellow daffodils were in bloom, and tiny, creamy-white crocuses and lapis-blue hyacinths had pushed their way through the soggy soil.

From our living room window, it was fascinating to watch the squirrels darting around the garden, trying to remember where they'd stashed their food at the beginning of winter. Ducks and geese dropped into the park, pecking and gobbling at the weeds caught in between the fence railings. Noisy, vivid-green parakeets were seeing off the sparrows, robins and magpies and hogging all the seeds left in the feeders hanging from the window of the top flat, of which I had a bird's eye view (couldn't resist the pun) from my sofa-vantage point. Spring was definitely around the corner.

One of the draws of London had been that our second son, Murdoch, was there. He'd come out to Teddington to see us the day after we landed and it had been the best feeling, putting our arms around him again.

Murdoch travelled with friends through Europe for several months, before settling in London in June 2014. He had an Ancestral Visa through Steve's mother (born in the UK) and was able to stay beyond the two years that limited most young people. These two years had to be completed before the age of

30. Murdoch initially took whatever job he could to pay the rent and feed himself, but ended up with an advertising company, working his way up to Assistant Creative Director, creating advertising campaigns and developing branding strategies for entertainment and sports brands.

One lazy Sunday, after wandering through the vibrant and newly-regenerated King's Cross area, we had a late lunch with Murdoch at Dishoom, a popular, classy Indian restaurant that he was keen to introduce us to. Unable to book, Steve and I joined the snaking queue at 1.30 p.m. and were told there was a wait of three-quarters of an hour. When Murdoch arrived, we'd reached third in line and we all agreed it was going to be worth the wait, judging by the number of Indian customers going in – and we were right. The food was absolutely scrumptious.

My interview with the dentist went well, but part of the role was some chair-side work. While working for Nigel Parr, an Auckland oral surgeon, I could only ever stand at the surgery door to speak to him while he was operating. Nigel was such a tease; he'd come up with some ploy to try to lure me across the threshold to stand beside him – like suddenly becoming deaf and not hearing what I was saying from the doorway. But I was never going to enter that surgery – I couldn't bear to see what was happening inside someone's mouth. So, the chair-side part wasn't going to suit me at all.

It was a private practice, and the dentist knew I only wanted to work two days a week. Having had a little taste of freedom already, it dawned on me after that interview that really, I didn't want to have an office job at all. I'd just be swapping my Auckland working life for another in London, and I was enjoying my new, freer, life very much already. But I did need to earn some money.

As for the interview to help the lady hosting a week-long house party at her *manoir* in Normandy, I got 'bumped' before I even got an interview! The lady decided to employ someone who was already in Normandy. I understood that and it did make perfect sense. So, it was back to the drawing board for me.

Steve's alarm woke us from our slumber at 6.00 a.m. one Monday morning. He had to be up early, get himself sorted and out the door to his course in Marble Arch. I heard the shower then nothing else, having fallen back asleep. Until: "Do you want a cup of tea before I go?" Steve whispered, waking me.

"Hm? Oh, no thanks. I'm going to doze a little longer. Hope it all goes well and I'll see you tonight," I murmured, pulling the covers up under my chin.

"Yes, see you." A peck on my cheek, and he was gone.

I rolled over lazily, luxuriating in the fact that all our necessary administration work had been completed and, with nothing further to be done, the day was mine – already planned and mapped out.

My destination was the elegant homeware boutique cum garden and greenhouse shop, café and restaurant known as Petersham Nurseries in Richmond. I'd heard and read about it, and it sounded just my sort of place.

Citymapper was uploaded on my phone and became my guide to getting around and finding my way home. I had the freedom to be able to walk and walk and not worry about the time or where I'd end up. Such a luxury.

In the village of Ham (the name comes from the Old English word Hamme meaning 'place in the bend of a river'), I noticed a wonderful German delicatessen called Hansel & Pretzel, which made me smile. I couldn't just walk past; I had to go in. Resisting the mouth-watering breads, pretzels, cakes and pastries was difficult, but I was saving myself to have a treat with my coffee at Petersham. I knew that Steve would be in heaven in Hansel & Pretzel. He could choose from the magnificent array of German sausages and cheese when we came back together.

Not too far on, I came across the lush green fields of the London (Ham) Polo Club. It's the last polo club in existence in London and has been around since 1926. Two young girls were on horseback returning to the stables after the morning exercise regime and, in the distance, I could see the magnificent, deep red brick of Ham House, which is now part of the National Trust. A visit was already in the diary for Easter.

Wending my way down dirt tracks and pathways, with high hedges and brick walls creating a tunnel effect either side of me, I emerged at Petersham Nurseries. The entrance was through high gates hung between two brick pillars, topped with stone urns. Turning in, I was immediately captivated.

It was like another world and unique, with compacted clay floors throughout all the rooms. The owners had saved a dilapidated and rickety nursery from a developer and turned it into a garden paradise and a cornucopia of bespoke homeware items. Its rustic beauty was its glamour. Here was a calming space in which to savour a delectable lunch sitting in the dappled light-filled greenhouse, surrounded by scented plants and potted palms that reached the ceiling. Ivy, woven between the fairy lights strung up under a huge greenhouse roofline, gave a luxurious and almost tropical feel.

Vases, age-spotted mirrors, tableware and giftware were displayed on distressed tables and other antique furniture and spilled out of aged armoires. The colourful and seasonal floral artworks were stunning, yet simplistic. These, and the Diptyque candles, scented the store with a heady fragrance and created a vision of luxury and loveliness.

I sat in the glasshouse tearoom, absorbing it all whilst having coffee and a freshly baked raspberry and lemon muffin, my head swivelling. The rustic theme continued there, with battered tin, metal and wooden tables and school-type chairs set out for customers to sit at.

In the garden shop, tiered, old wooden shelves were stacked with terracotta pots filled with pure white geraniums and vivid-green 'baby tears' planted up in baskets and nestled under frothy potted palms. The contrasting colours made a wonderful splash, with botanical greeting cards, gardening forks and gloves casually stashed in a wooden trug sitting beside them. Huge blue and white chinoiserie vessels, crammed with phalaenopsis orchids were clustered together in varying sizes on a bleached oak table and gave a nod to another era when grand houses with a conservatory would be filled with these. This place was heaven on a stick.

Dragging myself away, I wandered down the dirt lane and, from Petersham Meadow, looked up to see The Petersham, an elegant and regal hotel built in 1865, sitting in its commanding position on the hill, overlooking the bucolic landscape of Belted Galloways grazing in the fields, the flow of the Thames and the Thames Path. I wound my way up to the top of Richmond Hill, discovering the old MacKenzie Richmond Hill hospital which was closed in 2003 after an outbreak of SARS. It was being renovated into exclusive apartments and was architecturally beautiful, retaining its original clay-tiled roof, red-brick walls, ornate eaves, and cornice façade. After it was a hospital, it became the Star & Garter Hotel. From the advertising boards outside, the apartments looked luxurious ... and expensive.

I strolled down Richmond Hill towards the town, stopping to take in the views across the gentle turn of the glorious Thames through meadows and pathways, ancient stands of trees and also Richmond Park, with a glimpse of the spire of The Petersham. Further afield I could see the famous Twickenham Stadium but, no matter how hard I squinted, I couldn't see any turrets or flag flying at Windsor Castle which allegedly, could be seen from my spot. Behind me, running the length of the road, stood a sweep of Georgian houses, some double-fronted, but all so beautifully restored and elegant.

I knew I was going to have to come back for some proper exploration of the Richmond Hill boutiques. The most outstanding was the façade of Bramble & Moss, the flower shop. It's a graceful late-Victorian building, and so eye-catching with its deep green and olive-green tiles, gold paintwork and stained-glass window band, around the top quarter of the pavement-to-roof, rounded windows. Light fills the interior, showcasing the luscious plants and creative floral arrangements – all enhanced with feathers and fruits.

After three hours on my feet, I was glad to sink into a bus seat and head home. I was looking forward to getting in the door to toast and a steaming bowl of spicy pumpkin soup.

"You okay, Steve, if I leave you to your books?" I checked, pulling on my thick jacket and winding a scarf around my neck. It was a mucky, cold day but I was itching to get out and about.

"I'd much rather be out exploring too, but I have to get on with it," came the disgruntled reply. Steve shuffled his papers and looked up at me. "Where are you off to?"

"Bushy Park. I want to go and see the deer. Citymapper tells me it's only a twenty-minute walk from here, so that's easy. I'll be a couple of hours probably, with a stop at M&S in the High Street on the way back to grab some milk. See you soon." I planted a kiss on his cheek and made for the door. I felt sorry for Steve, having to work and not being able to share my discoveries. I'd get him out and about soon.

Bushy Park became a royal park in 1529 when Cardinal Wolsey gave it to King Henry VIII as part of a gift which also included Hampton Court Palace. A twelve-mile long man-made river was created in the park in the mid-seventeenth century as there was always a shortage of water at the palace. The Chestnut Avenue was designed by Sir Christopher Wren, and horse chestnut trees and a stand of lime trees line the mile-long walk leading to the Diana Fountain in the centre. This is not Princess Diana, but the goddess Diana, built in the 1630s and originally intended for Somerset House in London. During my first visit it was still winter and the trees in the avenue were stark and bare but still very imposing.

There is so much rich history attached to Bushy Park and, during the Second World War, part of the park became a US base, from where the Supreme Headquarters of the Allied Expeditionary Force, led by General Eisenhower, planned the D-Day Landings.

Hundreds of people use the park daily to exercise in and to walk their dogs, off leash. At every entrance to the park, notices abound about dogs worrying the deer and the fact that, if they are caught doing so, hefty fines will be imposed on the owners. These signs also warn that the deer are wild animals and people are to take great care whilst in the park, especially during the rutting season. During our time living in Teddington, we saw many foolish people getting too close, trying to feed them and to take pictures of their children beside the deer. It was plain crazy. Not surprisingly, people were attacked, and a child was gored and had to be air-lifted to hospital that first summer. This awful episode aside, I was so impressed with what was on our doorstep. There was just so much to see and do but several hours later I made tracks for home.

"Is the Fire Risk Assessor course any good?" I asked Steve, setting his cup of tea down beside his books.

"Yeah, I'm enjoying it. It's actually really interesting, but so much is just plain common sense. There's a lot of in-depth detail as well, that I need to absorb. When I spoke to Alan this morning, he said so much has changed, following the Grenfell Tower fire tragedy, and I'll probably have to complete another course in late April. I get that."

"God, you'll be at the desk for another couple of months at this rate," I sighed.

"Well, council laws for fire protection and risk have altered significantly since we first investigated this as a work option. According to Alan, even he, as a highly skilled assessor, must complete more course work to comply with the new regulations."

We decided to take things a week at a time and keep evaluating what we needed to do to enable us to stay and have a reasonable standard of living, as well as time to explore.

Not working gave me time to become a discerning shopper and Bridget put me onto Fish Fridays at Waitrose. All fresh fish was 20 per cent off, which was quite a saving. Steve was keen on a fish night, but I'm not great at cooking fish, so I approached the counter with a little trepidation. Not knowing the types of fish available didn't help.

The fishmonger behind the counter, with his white cotton apron straining across his ample middle, detected me dithering. He pushed his Union Jack-banded Panama hat back on his head, leaned forward, his forearms resting on the counter, and asked in a kindly voice, "Ow can I 'elp yer today, luv?"

"I'd like a cod fillet please. Enough for two," I ventured.

"Luvly. Would yer like me to cu' it in 'alf for yer, luv?"

"Um, yes thank you. Actually, I'm not very good with fish," I confessed, "what's the best way to cook cod?"

"Right, well I tell yer wot I'm gunna do, luv," he said. "I'm gunna put it in this 'ere bag, seal it and you just bung it straigh' in the oven; bag 'n all. Cooking times and temperatures are all on the back and I'll circle it for yer. Ow's that, luv, alrigh'? Now, free o' charge, wot garnishes would yer like? A bi' o' parsley and some lemon? 'Erb butter? Truffle butter?"

"Um, the parsley and lemon and, if it's okay, may I have a little herb butter too, please?"

"No problem a' all, luv. 'Ere yer go. I think yer really gunna enjoy that bi' o' cod. You 'ave a luvly day, luv. Cheerio."

"Thank you very much! You've been so helpful." I beamed at him, tucking my perfect little fish parcel into my basket.

Well, he was just a champion in my eyes, and I walked away with two lovely pieces of cod, all ready for me to 'bung in the oven'. Steve was 'gunna be dead chuffed' with me when I delivered steaming hot and perfectly cooked fish to the table, beautifully garnished with 'a bi' o' parsley, lemon and 'erb butter'!

Isn't that fantastic? I'd definitely go back there for another 'luvly' chat with my fishmonger.

At Waitrose, if I spent £10 or more, I also had a choice of a free newspaper *and* a free coffee – another little gem I discovered. I wrestled my coffee and over-stuffed bags to a seat provided by the store, off to the side of the check-outs, to rearrange everything for the bus ride home. A pleasant-looking older woman was already there drinking her coffee and, while I was repacking my purchases, we exchanged smiles and she spoke to me.

"You're juggling a bit there, dear," she said. "Will you manage it all?" I detected a foreign accent but needed to hear more to determine which it was.

"Oh, it's fine, really. I'm catching the bus across the road, down to Teddington. Then I'm a couple of minutes from home, so it's easy. But isn't it lovely to see the sun out today and it's that much warmer too."

"Well, I can tell you're not English!" she declared, and off we went, jabbering away, ten to the dozen.

One hour later, my bags repacked, coffees finished, phone numbers exchanged, I left the supermarket with a spring in my step. My new best friend, Maria, was Spanish (from Bilbao) by birth, had degrees in both Spanish and French, was widowed at 35, had only one child, was vivacious, hugely interested in art, books, theatre and passionate about her garden. I was booked in to have coffee at her place the following week and was so delighted.

"I had the best time at the supermarket this morning, Steve," I called out to him, hauling the shopping through the front door and kicking it shut behind me.

"Only you, Annemarie, could have the best time at the supermarket," he snorted, meeting me halfway down the hall. "What happened?" He took my bags, putting them on the kitchen bench. Unloading the shopping I explained all about meeting Maria and everything that had unfolded.

"Well done, Detective Inspector Rawson. You certainly got plenty of information out of Maria," he grinned stupidly at me. He always says I ask too many personal questions. It's so not true ...

I had to go out again later in the day and, while at Sainsbury's across the road, I found a favourite of Steve's – Terry's Chocolate Orange. I buy one for him every Christmas to leave under the tree. He always knows exactly what's inside, just by the shape of it. I squirrelled this one away in the back of the cupboard to produce with a great flourish at Easter. While I was at Sainsbury's there was a mix of six bottles of wine at 25 per cent off on offer. We might just have to take advantage of that too ...

"Do you feel up to going out? We could walk to Ham House," I suggested.

Steve had been laid low from a nasty flu bug he'd contracted during a week of classroom course work, which left him with a rattling, chesty cough. I'd never known Steve so sick, and I was glad he'd seen a doctor who'd diagnosed a virus, with no antibiotics required, just time, fluids and rest. He was fed up with being housebound. It had been painful for Steve even to talk. Luckily for him, there was nothing wrong with me in the 'talking' department ...

"Yeah, I think so. It would be good to get out," he rasped. He hadn't left the flat for days, so I made sure he was wrapped up warmly in his thick jacket and scarf and plonked a beanie on his head.

Ham House is one of many National Trust sites around the UK. The front gates sweep open to an elegant and opulent view of the gravel driveway and entrance, where brick walls curve inwards from both sides and stone busts are set inside charming oval alcoves and at symmetrical points, leading to the front steps. Topiarised trees and bushes create a formal scene.

A shaded sitting area, to the side of the front door, gives a long view out through the gates and down to the Thames. Imagine sitting there in the eighteenth century, watching the spectacle of promenading ladies in their beautiful silk dresses and matching parasols, strolling on a summer's afternoon along the water's edge.

The architecture is Jacobean; the property was built in a very attractive red brick in 1610 and it was still standing in 2018 – 400 years later. Incredible. The house is one of the great Stuart houses, situated only 10 miles from central London and was gifted to William Murray (an enterprising courtier) by King Charles I in 1626. Charles and William had been educated together as boys and had remained friends as adults. It was William and his daughter, Elizabeth, who transformed the place and it has remained the same since. Ham House is apparently a rare seventeenth-century survivor of luxury and grandeur.

Squares cut in the very tall hedges surrounding a side garden, created a 'window' to give a vista over the inner plots and potagers. During our visit fertiliser was being dug in, ready for planting. It would only be a matter of months before they became a carpet of spring flowers and vegetables. To have a vast and spacious lawn was always an indication of a landowner's wealth and William's was no exception. He obviously had land to spare, which didn't need to be cultivated for food or the grazing of stock, and the lawn ran from the back steps down to a hard-clipped hedge, away in the distance. Back in the day, a very skilled gardener was employed to keep the grass to a one-inch level – using a scythe. *Very* skilled indeed.

Elizabeth's enormous bathroom was situated in the basement with only a small fireplace and would have been as cold as charity. "It must have been freezing in this mausoleum of a bathroom," I muttered to Steve. "That fireplace wouldn't warm a block of ice."

"No, and imagine how long it would take to fill that bath. You'd need an army of servants, trundling back and forth from the kitchen with pails of hot water."

"No doubt they did have an army of servants," I agreed. "But look at that parquet floor, it's beautiful." There was such a skill to measuring out and laying the small timber cuts to create the distinctive, repeating pattern.

Numerous fire buckets hung on the walls in the hallway leading to the kitchens, as well as a long pole to unhook them. In the event of a fire, the staff would form a human chain from the house down to the Thames – approximately a third of a mile. I couldn't imagine this method would have salvaged much, but what else could they do?

The benefit of us touring in winter meant fewer people

about, but the downside was bare gardens and plants and statues 'winter-ised,' meaning they were covered to protect them during the very cold months. Sadly, the upper floors of the house were closed off as volunteers were waxing the floors and making repairs, prior to a mid-April opening.

Living in a one-bedroom flat, I needed to find somewhere nice close by for friends and family to stay. I was busy looking at B&Bs online and working out the distances from us. My eye was caught by the very attractive photos of a studio, which even had its own private little garden, set beyond French doors. The bathroom was huge and beautifully fitted out. Everything looked perfect. I Googled the address, discovering it was just a five-minute walk from our door. I did need to go and check it out though. I've been caught before, having looked at lovely photos only to find a place dirty and battered.

I messaged Anne, the owner, to ask whether it would be okay to pop round sometime, explaining I had terribly fussy friends and family. I only said that so she wouldn't think it was me. But of course, it *was* me – I'm just as bad!

Attractive large homes sat either side of the gravelled private lane leading to Anne's property. When I arrived on her doorstep, I could see hers was just as nice. As soon as Anne opened the door, I knew I'd found the right person and the right place.

"You must be Annemarie. Very nice to meet you. Come in," she said with a smile.

"Thank you. What a lovely home you have." My eyes were roaming everywhere, taking it all in. I was standing in a large, square, tiled entranceway with a bookcase to one side, the timbered staircase ahead of me and open doorways leading to a large kitchen, an office and a very welcoming sitting room.

Light filled the kitchen doorway, and I could see multi-paned French doors leading out to a large garden.

"The studio is just through here and, of course, whenever someone is staying it locks on the other side. There's a separate garden and private entrance via a footpath on the other side. I'll show you that shortly." Anne led me through a door on the left, just beyond the bookcase.

When I stepped into the studio, I really didn't need to go any further. I could see it would be very comfortable to stay in – spacious, with a king-sized bed that looked to have quality linen, bedside tables and reading lamps, a squishy two-seater sofa to read on, as well as a table to work from or eat at. Pretty, framed prints decorated the walls. Anne opened a set of bi-fold doors to reveal a super kitchenette with a little fridge, a two-burner hob, sink, microwave plus the usual kettle, cups and glasses. It was very well done and compact and all that anyone would need.

The French doors opened to a small private garden in which to sit and eat on a summer's evening.

The bathroom was enormous and, as well as the requisite shower, it also had a large bath. Fluffy towels were hanging over a heated towel rail, ready and waiting for the next guest. Everything was immaculately clean.

"Anne, this is just perfect, thank you." I turned, beaming at her. "Everything is so beautifully done. Thank you so much for showing me. My friends and family will be very comfortable here and only five minutes to me and two minutes to the High Street. It couldn't be better."

"You're very welcome. It was no bother at all." Anne closed the connecting door behind us.

I was at the front door, about to leave when she asked, "Are you in a hurry? Would you like to stay and have coffee?"

"Oh, I'm not in a hurry, no, and coffee would be very nice, thank you." How lovely.

"Great, come into the kitchen and I'll make us one. You're a New Zealander, aren't you?" she asked, popping the kettle on. "My brother lives in Blenheim and we've been to New Zealand, so I recognised the accent. Richard, my husband, and I lived in Sydney for a while and absolutely loved our time there. Oh wait ..." Anne turned to look at me, holding our empty coffee cups in mid-air. "Or are you Australian? I know there's great rivalry between the two countries so forgive me if I'm insulting you – one way or the other!" She laughed.

I laughed too. "Not at all. I have a very strong, plain accent and I've been asked if I'm Australian a few times, but you were right first time and those who have been to New Zealand usually pick it as that."

Just then, my attention was grabbed by two beautiful cats sunning themselves in a sliver of wintry, late-morning sunshine on the patio. One was a grey and white, fluffy-looking Persian and the other a very sleek and elegant black cat – no idea of breed. I love cats and just had to open the door to them. "Ooh, you've got cats! Is this okay, Anne? What are their names?" I was already halfway out the door.

"Of course it is, but they may run ..." She didn't get to finish her sentence before the two of them shot off under the bushes. I shut the door again, hugely disappointed.

"They can be funny with strangers at first, but I'm sure they'll come in to be nosy very soon. They are called Keith and Mick – Keith Richards and Mick Jagger."

Catching my raised eyebrows, Anne rolled her eyes, grinned and said, "Don't ask." She put the hot coffees down on the table between two comfy armchairs in the sitting room.

"Come and sit down and make yourself at home. I'm dying to hear how you came to be in Teddington. Well in the UK, really, and what your plans are."

An hour later we said farewell at the front door, with a drink date already set to meet at The Tide End pub (another pub around the corner from both of us) so Steve and Anne's husband Richard could meet. That was the start of a great friendship that would see us out and about with them at theatre, exhibitions, country pub lunches, visiting gardens and at theirs for dinners and vice versa.

Anne suggested that perhaps one way for me to meet people would be to join the Teddington Women's Institute (WI) – think *Calendar Girls* movie – which she had been meaning to do too. So we said we'd brave it together and check it out and if it seemed not too stiff and starchy, I'd join up. I'd be making cakes and jams and be on a stall fundraising for this, that and the other before you knew it. And don't get any funny ideas that I'd appear topless anytime soon on any calendar. *That* was most definitely not going to happen. Just so you know and don't ask...

The day I was exploring Bushy Park, Steve had been busy studying. I really wanted him to see the herds of deer scattered all over, so on our way to Hampton Court Palace, I walked him through it.

We pushed open the wrought-iron gates and stood, watching a green workhorse Range Rover being driven slowly along the pathways. A large herd of antlered deer cantered behind it. What a sight. They recognised the vehicle and could smell lunch. As soon as the park ranger hauled a big bag of goodies from the back of the wagon, he was surrounded as he tried to scatter the food on the ground whilst keeping clear of those antlers. Fabulous wildlife so close to home.

At the kiosk we stopped to pick up coffee before wandering through the gardens and over a little bridge, spanning a stream. Here, beautiful Egyptian geese with their glossy plumage and distinctive chocolate-brown 'eye patch' waddled along the edges, easing gently into the water. The birdlife, both in the trees and on the water, was prolific. I turned my phone on just to record the chorus and the woodpeckers, ratta-tat-tatting.

The park was a hunting ground for Henry VIII and, back then, ran for miles from the palace gates but now a road runs through the centre of it, dissecting the park from the palace and separating Teddington from East Molesey.

The magnificent Lion Gate on Hampton Court Road was our entry point into the Palace gardens. I wished someone would take soapy water and a scrubbing brush and get stuck into cleaning up some of these wonderful but filthy, dirt-engrained monuments that stand throughout London. I thought maybe that could be a wee job for me? This was yet another late-winter visit, but still beautiful as frothy pink blossom billowed from trees and early yellow daffodil faces danced in the light breeze. The front of the Palace reflected Ham House in terms of brick colour and pointing, but it wouldn't be until we got inside that we'd see its real beauty of rich oak panelling, and the stone stairs with scoops and dips from the footfall of kings, queens and servants over the centuries. Then there were the incredible ceilings – *trompe l'oeil* and hammer-beam being two of them.

It was Good Friday and supposed to be a Bank Holiday, but in the High Street it really was business as usual. All the shops, supermarkets, real estate agents and hairdressers were open. However, in Bushy Park and Hampton Court Palace Gardens, lots of families were making the most of the day off and enjoying themselves, with their energetic dogs racing across the fields, sniffing and greeting others in an excited frenzy. There's nothing like a good run in the park to exhaust dogs as well as little children. Both were having a ball and children squealed in delight, running around in colourful macs and brightly spotted/striped gumboots, stomping and splashing through puddles.

The entry to the children's Magic Garden is so attractive with its topiary in planter boxes. A clipped-yew arrow shape and a dog nestled in amongst the primroses. The Lindt Easter Bunny hunt was advertised for Easter Sunday, and I knew it would be mobbed, judging by the number of children there on a wet day.

Huge rectangular potagers had been freshly dug over with mulch, and pea, beetroot, kohlrabi and many other vegetable seedlings were bedded in. It would be a visual delight and a gourmet's feast, come midsummer when everything was ready. Espaliered, heritage fruit trees sprawled across the internal brick walls – mostly pear but each was done differently. Once a week during summer, the public could buy fruit and vegetables not needed for the café. I made a mental note of that, especially being within walking distance.

The timber weather-beaten gardeners' sheds were 'staged' to re-create the interior from over a century ago. Peering through the windows, I could see old gardening implements hung on the walls, coils of rope and string draped on rusty hooks and ancient and faded seed packets stacked upright in a column in an old wooden trug. Books, written in perfectly formed calligraphy, recording all the planting and harvesting, lay open on a battered and scrubbed pine table, and a capped fountain pen rested in the binding of one. A well-chewed pipe, tobacco and matches sat in a dish to one side. I imagined how it must smell inside – of earthy, rich soil and dense, sweet and spicy tobacco smoke. To complete the picture, old terracotta pots were stacked up on a couple of shelves lining one wall and worn and ripped gardening gloves hung over the edge.

The rain was starting to pelt down and after our three hours of walking, I pushed my brolly up, looped my arm through Steve's and hustled us to the bus stop, not wanting him to get wet and sick again.

March Snippets

Win a dinner. We hadn't even been in Teddington a month when I correctly answered a question on a local radio station and won a three-course dinner for two plus a bottle of wine at The Wharf Restaurant – a short walk from our driveway and right on the Thames. I was tickled pink. They even interviewed me live. It was such a great welcome to Teddington, and they made a big song and dance about us moving there from New Zealand. The question was: what rice is used for creating a risotto – arborio or basmati? Do you know? It's an easy question for someone who cooks.

But I did have to think *very* hard about who I'd take to dinner with me ...

Richmond. With the freedom to get on and off as much public transport as we liked, we bussed down to Richmond one March Sunday morning for coffee. Everybody loves Richmond. It's an historic town and a slice of heaven, with a vast royal park bursting with wildlife, pleasure craft bobbing on a bend of the Thames, a fabulous eighteenth-century stone arched bridge, and stunning Georgian architecture. People lined the riverbank, drinking coffees and chatting, just enjoying a magnificent weekend morning.

The town itself is a cluster of offices, pubs and high-end boutique shops intersected with lots of alleyways and lanes and cafés and restaurants. We chanced upon a great café and had superb coffee. One of the girls on the counter was from Somalia and had come to the UK as a baby. When she discovered we were New Zealanders she stamped her foot, saying, "I'm always telling mum off for not choosing New Zealand." She laughed and explained, "Twenty-five years ago, she and dad pored over a map of the world, deciding where to emigrate. But it was here, the UK, where they ended up. And it's been fine but now, as an adult, I wish it had been New Zealand. It's so beautiful."

"One reason might be because even today, so many maps don't show New Zealand, so that could easily have been the case back then," Steve pointed out.

"Maybe," she pondered, "but tell me, why are New Zealanders so friendly?"

I couldn't really answer that at the time, but thinking about it later, my conclusion was that we have such a sense of freedom and feel no personal threat from anyone.

The following link will take you directly to photos associated with March. Feel free to comment on any of them.

https://bit.ly/LLA_March-2018

APRIL 2018
SOUTHBANK; BRIXTON; COUNTRY LIVING FAIR; BOMBER COMMAND

Part of Steve's course work was to complete a fire risk assessment report on a complex building. The Anglers pub around the corner was the perfect place, with its large commercial kitchen, staff accommodation, several function rooms and being on three levels. Luckily, we'd built up a good rapport with the two barmen (what does that tell you?) and one of them went off to check with his boss if it was okay for Steve to assess the pub and, if so, to make an appointment. It was not a problem and the report was duly completed and submitted.

Steve's focus then was to knuckle down and revise all the course work in preparation for his exams later in the month. He hadn't been told how long it would be before he got his results, but he needed to be proclaimed 'competent' before anyone would employ him. Even then, it was going to be difficult, as all the jobs now advertised wanted people with experience. Nevertheless, once his exams were out the way he would begin chasing work. The whole process was taking forever, and it could easily be the end of May before he got work. I was continually looking at Seek in the evenings and on local sites for work for myself too. It was all getting a bit worrying with nothing jumping out at us.

On a brighter note, we loved being there, under grey skies or in sunshine. There was so much to see and do and it was hard to choose what next. While Steve completed his pub assessment report on Easter Saturday, I took a train into the Tate Modern, walking from Waterloo station and getting amazing glimpses between buildings of the impressive Shard, soaring into the sky.

The Tate Modern gallery is housed in the imposing façade of the 1947 Bankside Power Station and, once the new addition opened in 2021, it would house even more diverse international modern and contemporary artworks. I only explored the standard exhibitions – many of which I couldn't get my head around – but all the rooms were humming with lots of tourists in London for that Easter weekend.

The gallery sits directly opposite the centuries-old St Paul's Cathedral on the other side of the river, connected by the Millennium Bridge. I'd never walked over it before, so I joined the throng of people crossing on that very cold day, hunched into my coat with the collar turned up and gloved hands thrust deep into my pockets. The sickly-sweet aroma of roasted, caramelised nuts sold from a cart strategically placed at the entrance to the bridge on the St Paul's side, was reeling in tourists and the seller was doing a roaring trade. I did fancy something hot, but not those.

The dipping sun, several hours walking and the thought of a cup of hot tea were enough to send me looking for the nearest bus back to Waterloo station and home.

Murdoch rang one Monday morning. "Mum, what are you and Dad doing on Friday? I've got the day off but need to catch up on some admin at home so thought you might like to come and have lunch here. See where I live."

Murdoch lived in Brixton in the borough of Lambeth, South London – described as a bohemian neighbourhood, bursting with art, music, culture and fabulous food. It's a multi-ethnic mix of people but mainly African-Caribbean, which brings with it a riot of colour, exotic markets and always great music.

"Love to, Murdoch. Dad and I haven't got anything booked. I'll make a bacon and egg pie to bring, and we can warm it through in your oven. Will that do?" I suggested.

"Great. Thanks mum. Come mid-morning and we'll have coffee first at my local, Brixton Blend. It's excellent and just across the road from the tube station. You can't miss the David Bowie mural and the café is opposite that. See you Friday."

Sadly, Brixton's name became synonymous with the riots that took place in 1981 and the song 'Electric Avenue' by Eddy Grant, is about the street around the corner from the tube with the same name. It began life in the 1880s and was the first market street to be lit by electric lights. This lively avenue is now full of food and vibrant clothing markets.

Standing at the top of the stairs at Brixton tube station I could have been in Jamaica, not a suburb of London. It was so intoxicating. Throngs of people in all sorts of exotic dress and colourful headgear, some with the customary dreadlocks, surged along the pavement threading their way through to the markets, shops and the station. Two guys were on kettle drums, belting out some great music, their heads swaying and feet tapping in time. It was infectious and I found myself jigging away to the rhythm while we waited for Murdoch.

Brixton Blend cafe's décor was very cool and rustic. The underside facing of the counter was constructed from multi-coloured, painted top halves of old front doors, complete with glass fan lights, brass door knockers, letterbox flaps, keyholes and street numbers. It was clever, very different and great recycling.

"Grab that table next to the window," Murdoch pointed, coming through the door. "You'll get a great view of the David Bowie mural. I'll get the coffees."

We settled in with Murdoch, our coffees and pastry treats, while he told us a little about the mural. "Dad, you'll know that Bowie was born here in Brixton, right?" Steve nodded, his mouth being full of almond croissant. "Well, the mural was paid for by a James Cochran in 2013 and, when Bowie died in January 2016, people came here, standing six feet deep, some with their faces painted just like that," he nodded at the mural, "some holding lit candles and all paying their respects, leaving flowers and messages. As time went on, the mural became tatty with people writing messages over the artwork. So it was decided to get it repainted and put a protective plastic over it. Sadly, that too became a mess with writing and stickers so now it has that Perspex cover, and it seems to have worked as it hasn't been defaced at all."

Murdoch sipped at his hot coffee and continued, "Hardly a day goes by, on my way to the tube, that I don't see a bunch or small posy of flowers left there. Good ol' Bowie. He lives on for so many people."

"He was definitely a very talented man and obviously still sorely missed by so many," said Steve, taking in the colours and mural artwork.

"And did you know there's a great pop-up store here selling New Zealand wines? It's fantastic. Called New Zealand Cellars, it's run by Melanie Brown. You'll like this mum. She's a New Zealand chef as well as a true wine buff. Apparently, she's worked with Raymond Blanc, Jamie Oliver, and our own Peter Gordon – just to name a few – and she also owns The Laundry, a cool bistro and wine shop not far from here. It actually did used to be a laundry. You'll be wanting to stop at the Cellars on your way back and pick up a Central Otago red." Murdoch winked and nudged me.

"Wow. She's done well for herself. Good on her. I love to hear Kiwis' overseas success stories," I said. "Hm, maybe we will stop in there for a look."

"C'mon." He stood, draining his coffee cup. "You two done? We'll make tracks to my place."

His home was only a five-minute walk from the tube so was in a very handy location. However, I don't think I have ever been in such a small flat. It suited him just fine though and he'd lived there for two years with two male flatmates – one of whom owned it. From the outside, it was a large and typical two-storeyed terraced house that was split in two, but when Murdoch opened the front door there were another two doors that were effectively front doors to the flats immediately in front of us. Half the house had been split in half again! Bizarre, but this was not uncommon in dense housing areas like Brixton.

In the half of the half where Murdoch lived, there were three bedrooms, a tiny living area, a tiny but perfectly functioning kitchen and, down a flight of stairs (in the basement) was a modern bathroom. It was great to see where he lived and, of course, we loved now being in the same city and spending time with him.

I did wonder if we would miss having a car but we could categorically say no, we didn't. Everything we needed was on our doorstep. It was a twelve-minute walk to the train, which was easily do-able and the bus was a three-minute walk. Making several connections from one mode of transport to another was a breeze and very rarely did we wait more than a few minutes. It worked brilliantly for us.

Not having a car did mean I shopped for groceries several times a week, nearly always taking with me Cruella de Vil, the aptly named Dalmatian-spotted and trendy shopping trolley Irene kept stowed in the hall cupboard. I never thought I'd be wheeling a trundler around but so many people of all ages used them, and I just blended in. I'd trot Cruella down to Aldi in Kingston-Upon-Thames and get the bus back with my bulging trolley. It was far easier to pull my shopping along behind me than to carry it.

Often, the postman arrived, calling a cheery good morning, when I was heading down the driveway. The Royal Mail service was still very much an institution, delivering six mornings a week, compared to New Zealand where mail deliveries were three times a week. When I first came to London in 1981, they delivered *twice a day*. The first delivery was early morning and, with no email or cell phones in those days, my then New Zealand flatmates and I would rush to the front door, hoping for letters from home, before we hurried off to work. We three girls were astounded to have two mail deliveries a day and it wasn't until 2004 that the early morning delivery was scrapped in the UK. In our flat in 2018 it tickled me to hear our mail flap rattle and the 'thunk' of letters dropping on the carpet. There were no mailboxes in the lobby and our postie climbed the stairs to everyone's door, leaving his little red cart locked in the car park. The posties must be quite fit as I didn't see any of them using the electric buggies they have in New Zealand.

I had a job! No, not with the dentist. I never did hear back from him. I was to project-manage renovation work on a one-bedroom basement flat in Shepherd's Bush. I'd also be the cleaner, accessories buyer and home-stager; getting the flat ready for sale. The owner was a woman in Wellington, New

Zealand called Caroline. She'd returned to New Zealand several years earlier, leaving the flat rented out. It was now on the market, but just wasn't generating any buyers. Caroline decided it needed work and wanted someone she could trust with her money and who would ensure that a quality finish was achieved. The easiest way to describe our relationship was that she was a family friend, but one I'd never met. We introduced ourselves over the phone and had an instant rapport. From then on, emails flew back and forth until the job was completed.

I collected the key from Caroline's estate agent and went to evaluate what needed doing. A pervading smell of damp greeted me as soon as I pushed the door open. The flat hadn't been lived in for six months. *Well, that's the first job to tackle* I thought, with a wrinkle of my nose. This job was right up my alley, and I was excited to be getting started. My Excel spreadsheet filled fast with what needed to be done, tradesmen to be engaged and all intended purchases. Caroline had given me an excellent budget to work with and I sourced recommended contractors and accessories.

My online portfolio, with photos showing the flat as it was, and updated as I made progress, would be useful for future work. If Caroline was satisfied, she would then be happy to recommend me to her estate agent and others. She thought there must be lots of absentee landlords/owners who wanted to sell but didn't know anyone they trusted to oversee the remedial work and to 'dress' a property ready for sale.

Since finishing work for Nigel Parr in Auckland, my confidence in my ability to work in an office or surgery had ebbed. There was very little work advertised that I felt qualified for, and it was my impression that most advertisers wanted that 'gorgeous young thing' at reception, who was on a career path, happy to work Saturday mornings and do late nights, often on a rotating roster. *No thanks.* Also, when I looked in the mirror and saw the wrinkles, I was reluctant to apply for the jobs that even slightly related to my skills. I think the overriding factor was my hesitancy to get caught up in the 9–5 (plus) of an office working life. I would only be swapping my Auckland working life for another, and that wasn't why we were there. So, project-managing renovations and creating a 'silk purse out of a sow's ear' on a part-time basis, was the sort of work I truly wanted. It was exhilarating and I threw myself into it.

Anne and Richard started filling our social calendar and our first meet-up at the Tide End pub had been a successful introduction for Steve and Richard. There was never a lull in the conversation and Richard promptly booked Steve in for golf and the regular Monday evening drinks with his friends at The Builders Arms (just off the High Street). Anne booked me in to have coffee at The Lensbury, the club where she swims and exercises, and to introduce me to several of her friends.

I went for coffee with Maria, my delightful Spanish new best friend, at her home in Kingston and had the loveliest time. I invited her to come to ours but, without a lift, she knew she'd have difficulty with the stairs. No matter. We arranged to meet again in the café at John Lewis in a couple of weeks. She was great fun and full of life and I was looking forward to seeing her again. There wasn't time to get lonely and Steve and I hadn't killed each other – yet.

The sun was rising earlier each day and, dare I say it, the air was a smidgen warmer. Spring was starting to spring, with the trees in the park next door blooming pink and white blossom, while lime-green shoots were budding on others. Birds flitted hither and thither, hurrying to finish their nests before babies arrived, scouting under the hedges for dried grasses, pecking mosses from trees and collecting fresh grass clippings as soon as the gardeners left.

I managed to coerce Steve into closing his books for a few hours on a relatively warm and sunny Saturday morning to come with me to Borough Market, to meet up with visiting New Zealand friends and to walk beside the Thames down Southbank. The market is easy to reach from Waterloo station and was heaving when we arrived at 10.00 a.m.

Coffee done and dusted, our friends headed off to an early theatre play and we joined the masses back in the market. This was my kind of heaven. Beautiful fresh fruit and vegetables, almost colour-coded, and cheeses so artistically stacked in wheels and wedges and lusciously presented; was all done to encourage people to taste then buy. The fish stall was another feast for the eyes – bright-eyed, whole fish, fillets, mussels and crayfish, while the oysters, glistening in their shells sitting on ice and surrounded by lemon quarters, were huge (just not for me!). With the traders shouting their wares, exotic meats barbecuing, people jostling for space with coffees and food in hand, it was a noisy, bustling, hunger-inducing atmosphere. It was so hard to choose what to have for lunch, but we nailed it down to spicy Cajun chicken burgers. So good!

Unable to find a seat we ambled our way back to Southbank, chewing as we went, enjoying the sun and warmth. The gorgeous day had brought so many people out and we were jostling for space in the narrower parts of the walk beside the river. How do you know it's a beautiful, warm spring London day? Because so much creamy and milky-white skin is on display – girls and women were in shoestring tops and shorts, mini dresses, or strapless dresses. Some of the men had donned the perfect white tee shirt to go with their shorts or jeans and trainers, looking very trendy.

I never tired of this part of London with views of Blackfriars Bridge, St Paul's Cathedral, the Shard, the Walkie Talkie, the

London Eye and many other significant London landmark buildings. It's an incredible variety of architecture and historic sights. There's always an abundance of life on the Thames – watercraft plying up and down and often we'd see people, known as mudlarks, with their metal detectors down on a small piece of muddy sand, exposed at low tide, looking for ancient and valuable treasure.

Home again and, our afternoon cuppa and Hobnob biscuit in hand, we scooted down the stairs, crossed the lawn and passed through the gate in the fence to sit on 'our' bench seat beside the river. It was still wonderfully warm, and the river here too was busy with people paddle-boarding, tootling about in dinghies or waving from the boats making their way upriver through the lock system. Looking up at our flats I could see everyone, including us, had flung their windows wide, releasing the winter stuffiness and welcoming in the warm spring air.

One unusually hot April day I met up with Mary. She and Symon, the couple we had worked for near Gaillac in France, lived in central London. Since our time in France, where we needed to maintain that fine line of employer/employee, we'd become good friends. Each time we had visited London since our return to New Zealand from France, we'd been lucky enough to get together with them at their home for drinks and dinner.

That morning, I left home at 9.00 a.m. and walked back in the door, shattered, at 8.15 p.m. I'd already done a quick-step walk with Steve first thing and when Mary checked her phone that evening, walking me back to Sloane Square to catch the train, we'd completed just on 11,000 steps.

No get-together with Mary ever starts without the

obligatory coffee. It's necessary, in order to get most of the chat out of the way. There's always an awful lot to talk about and catch up on. Mary and Symon have a son and a daughter, both the same ages as our two sons. Several years ago, Murdoch ventured out to Gaillac on his way through Toulouse and was fêted with lunch and a tour of the house and grounds Steve and I'd cared for. Since Murdoch's visit, he too had been lucky enough to join us for our get-togethers with Mary and Symon.

After a delay on the South Western train and rushing for tubes, it was good to finally hug Mary hello and plonk myself down, pour a large glass of water and order a reviving coffee. We met at a smart café, Comptoir Poilâne, in Cadogan Gardens – a light and airy space with appetising English and European provisions displayed on counter tops and wooden shelving, and serving great coffee.

After an hour of non-stop chat, we set out for The Royal Academy of Arts to view the Charles I exhibition. The Academy (more commonly known as the RA) is based in Burlington House, Mayfair and was originally a Palladian mansion, owned by the Earl of Burlington before being purchased by the government. As can be imagined, the interior architecture of the house is worthy of a visit on its own. Steve and I were yet to purchase our Art Fund card, but Mary belonged to every possible gallery and museum in London and was able to take a friend in at any time. I was that lucky friend.

In 29 °C stuffy, London heat, we moved on to Trafalgar Square and into The National Portrait Gallery. Even though Steve and I'd visited this gallery a few times, there was always a different exhibition to see. Portraits of the Queen, Prince Philip, and Diana are so life-like, and the ones of William and Harry so real, they were almost with us in the room.

By 2.00 p.m., hunger got the better of us. Mary whisked us up the elevator to the brightly lit Portrait restaurant on the top floor. Our window seats gave an expansive and marvellous view over the city, sadly punctuated at various points by cranes and scaffolding. London was in a frenzy of building activity.

Our colourful and tasty quinoa salads arrived, accompanied by water only. The rest of the day was ahead of us, and we couldn't afford to be stumbling through it in a wine-induced fog. Time was marching on. We bussed back to Mary's place for a cup of tea and a breather before our 5.30 p.m. visit to a Decorative Antiques and Textiles Fair at Battersea Park.

Even with the windows open, the bus was airless and sweltering. Central London had ground to a standstill with the Commonwealth Heads of Government Meeting taking place in its midst. The buses backed up, one behind the other, and the cacophony of endless traffic, fumes, people and police seemed so much worse in the heat. The cool and calm of Mary's kitchen was a haven to walk into and we received a joyous, bouncing and barking reception from the very gorgeous Penelope, the family Pekinese. What a bundle of fluff and affection. I was delighted when she snuggled in on my lap.

Copious cups of tea and water later, we were off again. First, to Mary's son and daughter-in-law's place. This was another gorgeous home. The daughter-in-law is very talented, creating a beautiful space with lamps, console tables, plants and artwork. Lots of fine art, but with more modern and contemporary, large works blended seamlessly with the old. All cleverly orchestrated.

This was my first time in Battersea Park, a 200-acre Victorian park, built between 1854 and 1870. The riverside promenade is a beautiful place to stroll or cycle. So many people were catching the late sun, enjoying a picnic dinner and sharing a bottle of something. The park also hosts a children's play area and zoo and it was popular and busy on such a warm, balmy evening. The Fair was brilliant. Mary and I fell in love with many French pieces up for sale – old armoires, battered shutters, wrought-iron gates and ornate gilt mirrors that were a little rusted, and paint-chipped. Everything exuded life and a history of France.

"Ooh, look! The drinks are heading our way," Mary exclaimed. A young man, beautifully kitted-out in a smart black suit, crisp white shirt and black bow tie was artfully pouring drinks from a heavily laden trolley, the bottles jiggling and clinking as he made his way between exhibits. "Let's have a little reviver. It's been a big day. Glass of champagne, Annemarie?"

"Love to. We've drowned in cups of tea and water today. My treat." I pulled my purse out.

As soon as he opened his mouth, I knew this charming young man was a New Zealander too. He was on his OE (overseas experience) year, living temporarily in London and earning a little money as a waiter. We enjoyed a bit of chat and banter while poor Mary was choking *before* she'd had a drop to drink. She'd seen the price. Mary started to waver, so this charming young man said to me, "Well, since we are from the same 'hood' you two can have a glass each at half price." What a sweetie. The glasses were firmly clasped in our hands before you could say 'Bob's Your Uncle' and the aromatic, yeasty champagne fizzed over our tongues, sliding down very easily.

It was gone 7.15 p.m. by the time we came out into the evening light and time for me to head home. Hugs and kisses exchanged, we arranged for Mary and Symon to come to Teddington for a walk along the Thames Path and a gastro pub lunch. Steve and Symon could then catch up and Mary and I would once again pick up where we left off ...

The Groupon website is a terrific place to find bargains and I was delighted to pick up a free ticket to the Country Living Spring Fair. This annual fair is associated with *Country Living*

magazine. It's a magazine to drool over, with interesting features and gorgeous food, furniture and décor for sale and the country lifestyle portrayed always looked idyllic. While Steve beavered away at his second and final exam, I took myself off to the fair at Alexandra Palace – known to every Londoner as Ally Pally. I'd never been out that way before, nor seen the Palace and, while on the train chatting with the woman next to me I asked, "Do you know what that beautiful building is up there?" I pointed out of the window to this extraordinarily grand place, sitting on a hill.

"Oh yes," she said, "that's Alexandra Palace. Well, it's also known as The People's Palace. I'm going to the Country Living Fair which is on there today."

"Oh, me too!"

"Well, I do hope you have your credit card with you because there's an awful lot to tempt you to buy," she laughed.

Just then we arrived at the station, both of us standing to get off. One of the ladies behind us said, "We're going to the Fair too, isn't it exciting!"

I then noticed a large group of women alighting onto the platform, all waiting to board the shuttle bus to the Palace and the Fair. The bus seemed full of flitting, colourful butterflies such was the hype and chatter of the women on our short distance to the Palace and all that awaited us behind the swing doors.

The place was fizzing and alive with people, music, chat and mouth-watering aromas. Everyone received a goodie bag of samples, which I tucked away for later. I was too busy taking everything in to be delving into it then. Booths and stalls were beautifully arranged, designed to lure people in to buy luxurious linens, cashmere, scented candles, artisan foods, handmade jewellery, classic homeware, organic beauty products, *faux* flowers and food. And more!

Wicker baskets, artfully arranged on stalls, were

overflowing with condiments, bottled fruits, jams and sauces and pretty floral napkins. Potted palms and plants surrounded wooden wheelbarrows filled with flowering white geraniums and lush green ferns. Everything oozed class and loveliness.

The famous Annie Sloan was conducting a chalk paint workshop and I was lucky to have a chat and my photo taken with her. She is such a talented lady. Further along, Viking Cruises handed me a glass of champagne, while regaling me with the virtues of their magnificent ocean and river cruises. As soon as I divulged we'd sailed on the Viking Homelands cruise through the Baltic, my glass was instantly topped up. It would have been rude to say no ...

There was also an area set up like a barn, with hay bales and straw strewn about. Three lambs were bleating away, huddled up with their mum, while chickens pecked, scratched and clucked away. I even got to cuddle one.

By lunchtime, The Gin Trailer was doing a roaring trade, not only offering a wide variety of gins and sporting a huge glass bowl of glossy yellow lemons on the counter, but also prosecco and ice creams. There was an ever-increasing queue.

I was stopped in my tracks at one stall, by a man dressed in his product – a suit made from vibrant and colourful outdoor striped fabric. He should have been called Jacob, wearing that technicolour suit. Nothing brings spring into your home like bright, striped fabric does.

April Snippets

Work. In amongst my comings and goings I managed to pick up another job working with a woman called Jamie. She lived in a beautiful old house near Windsor and was a talented chef (cordon bleu and Prue Leith-trained). Jamie was a busy woman and a little overwhelmed with what needed doing. I'd be helping her re-organise her home and her life and doing food prep for clients. Our first job together was to set her kitchen back up after a renovation, throwing out old stuff, making lists of what was needed and finding the appropriate home for everything Jamie wanted to keep. She was very bubbly, lots of fun and talked non-stop. Obviously, a kindred spirit ...

Maltby Street Market, Bermondsey/London Bridge. We met Murdoch here for a bite on the run. A great variety of foods, juices, beers and wine available from the 1836 viaduct portals. It was difficult to choose what to eat with all the intoxicating aromas wafting through the busy walkway. The London Marathon was on, the street was a throng of people and it was hard to get through the press. Londoners were loving the hot day ... half-naked bodies sprawled everywhere in the parks.

Bomber Command Memorial – Green Park. Dedicated to the 55,000 plus airmen who lost their lives during the Second World War. I have seen this a few times now and it never fails to move me. It really is a beautiful sculpture and captures the airmen so well. My dad was a gunner in the war and this is exactly how he would have been dressed, ready to walk out to the aircraft.

Her Majesty's Household Cavalry. I was waiting to cross from Hyde Park to Green Park when traffic stopped and the air echoed with the clip-clop of majestic black horses beautifully kitted-out, rounding the Wellington Arch. The Household Cavalry is regarded as the most prestigious in the British Army. The soldiers' plumed helmets, elegant uniforms and shining breastplates make them instantly recognisable. It was so fabulous to see them.

Having a drink in Anne's (B&B) garden. During this bout of warm, balmy weather, sitting amongst her tulips and spring growth colours of the burgundy-red and lime-green maple trees was so relaxing. A beautiful, purple lilac tree was in full bloom. Mick and Keith (Anne's cats – not the Rolling Stones) were lying in the shade and sprawled out on the still-warm pavers, adding to the ambiance and charm of the garden.

The following link will take you directly to photos associated with April. Feel free to comment on any of them.

https://bit.ly/LLA_April-2018

MAY 2018

CHARTWELL, KENT;
NORTHAMPTONSHIRE; OSTERLEY
HOUSE, LONDON; SKY GARDEN,
LONDON

I'd been planning to visit Churchill's home, Chartwell in Kent, for quite some time, but the weather and my work commitments had got in the way. However, Friday dawned with a clear blue sky and tantalising sunshine and the decision was made that today was the day. The bluebell season in the woods around Chartwell was coming to an end and if we didn't go then, we'd miss them altogether.

I quickly stuffed sandwiches, fruit and water into our backpack, handed it to Steve and we closed the door behind us at 7.30 a.m. It was a two-and-a-half-hour journey to Westerham, the closest village to Chartwell. One bus, tube, train and another bus ride later, we arrived to a busy morning full of sunshine, locals and tourists, on Westerham's village green, drinking coffee or tucking into breakfast, at the outdoor tables of the many cafés lining the street. Steve and I joined them, loving the warm sunshine on our backs and our own coffee.

Westerham is a pretty village sporting many clothing boutiques, antique shops and homeware. I had a lovely time window-shopping and several shops enticed me in. One was an interiors shop, filled with gorgeous French country décor. There were terracotta pots filled with herbs, large *faux* blooms of hydrangeas nestling in square wicker baskets, linens spilling out of the open vintage armoires, botanical prints, trailing ivy, scented candles and fluffy towels folded neatly into an alcove. I was in heaven.

Steve finally found me and poked his head in the door. "Have you finished? We need to get moving." He checked his watch. "We've got a bit of a hike through the woods, apparently. I've just asked in the café."

I took one last wistful look around the shop before I stepped back into the glaring sunshine, pulling my sunglasses off my head and back onto my nose. We'd already stripped off our jackets and Steve stuffed these into the backpack, ready to set off.

Forty-five minutes later, after a gorgeous warm, woodland walk where dappled light filtered through the new, leafy growth and a final tramp down a long track, we emerged into the car park area of Chartwell. I was so excited to be there and couldn't wait to get inside. We'd registered at the gate, received our allotted timeslot and, with passes and maps in hand, we wandered the beautiful gardens until we could enter the house.

The elevated distant views of the rolling hills and pastures were breathtaking, as were the immediate manicured gardens and lawned areas. Some fields had been left to grow wild. The kitchen garden was being planted up and tended while we looked on, but the hot pink and blood-red azaleas were already in full bloom, giving such a 'pop', nestled in the greenery. The pink and white cherry blossom was just announcing itself, promising an abundant crop in the summer.

At 12.20 p.m. we positioned ourselves, with a few other eager beavers, at the front door. The rooms were not large, hence the time allotment. It would be impossible to see anything or enjoy the rooms with hordes of people all pushing through. I last visited Chartwell when I was 23 and only remembered the exterior – built in old red brick, with a high-pitched roof and a two-storey entrance. A great expanse of lawn flowed from the front of the house, surrounded by a long, semi-circular high brick wall, topped at various points with concrete balls. Protected from the wind, this area had its own microclimate and, at precisely measured distances, large garden benches sat waiting to receive resting visitors or those just wanting to sit and admire the house.

Chartwell exuded comfort and it would have been very easy to settle into one of the squishy, fringed armchairs with a glass of wine in the drawing room or seated at the dining room table for tea and scones. One of the room guides was very welcoming and had a lovely warmth about her. We got talking.

"How long have you been here, then?" I asked.

"Not long. Twenty-three years," she gave me a wink.

"Gosh, that's so long!" I was quite stunned. "You must know the house history backwards by now, and everything there is to be discovered about the Churchills."

"Oh yes, I've got a bit of knowledge," she smiled, modestly. "It's special here. At the end of one season, all the guides were invited into the drawing room to sit, enjoy drinks and exquisite canapés, prepared especially for us." Her eyes almost misted over as she continued: "It was as if Clementine and Winston were in the room too, amongst the memorabilia. The house is so homely. It sort of wraps itself around you. Do you know what I mean?"

"Oh yes, I know exactly what you mean," I agreed. Standing there, looking at all the books lining the inset bookcases, the lamps, chandeliers and pretty floral drapes, I too could feel the warmth and history of the room.

"It's a lovely job and I never tire of showing the house off," she concluded. "Lovely chatting with you and enjoy the rest of your visit." She patted me on the arm. "Make sure you get down to Winston's studios. You'll have to excuse me, but I need to speak with the next group."

"Thank you!" I called to her departing back.

Another guide said that Churchill was not allowed to live there during the war because of the possibility that Chartwell might become a German air target. He went on to say that it had been stated by Goering's family that the Luftwaffe was instructed never to bomb Chartwell as Goering intended it to be one of his homes after the German invasion. All these snippets really made our visit special. One woman in our group quipped that she would have been quite happy to be Prime Minister if it meant living at Chartwell whilst running the country during the war.

Stunning landscape, still-life and portrait paintings adorned most walls, and I would have happily given a home to any one of the landscapes. Only a few were done by Churchill; the rest were by other accomplished artists.

One hallway was wallpapered in the prettiest floral paper, which not only covered the walls, but the ceiling and backs of doors too. It was original, over the top, but certainly effective.

Four rooms in the house were a museum, containing all Churchill's medals, uniforms, gifts, paintings and many photos of prime ministers, presidents, army generals and great friends. Everything made for interesting viewing and reading. A very special place in the house was in the basement, where a whole room was dedicated to Clementine, Churchill's wife. What a remarkable woman she was. Even though I'm speculating that Churchill dallied elsewhere in all their years together, she was his life and backbone, and vice versa. I did think Clementine needed to be fêted more publicly.

Coming out into the sunshine, we looked for a shady spot to have lunch before we explored the studio, where Churchill created so much. Painting was his relaxation and his favourite pastime. He produced over 500 paintings during his lifetime, had a natural talent and was basically self-taught. Walter Richard Sickert and William Nicholson, well-known artists of the day, were in his social circle, and he often sought their advice. His studio was bursting, with all four walls covered in many of his works.

It was soon time to return to Westerham and start our journey home. Patches of the pretty bluebells swayed in the warm breeze, but really not enough to create a decent carpet. We were a bit late and had missed them at their best. At a fork in the path, we weren't sure which way to go. Ahead of us a man was walking his two dogs, so I called to him: "Excuse me! Can you tell us which is the quickest path back to the village?" Hearing my voice, he turned around.

"Up here and over the rise takes you right into the middle of the village," he pointed. "C'mon. Follow me."

We quickly caught up and he introduced us to his two cute Westies – Archie and Millie. I chatted with him until we crested the hill where the rolling view silenced me – bright yellow fields of rapeseed were a vibrant pop of colour in the verdant green landscape. Towards the village, stone country cottages with their brick chimneys were tightly knitted together, along with tall church spires and steeples, drawing my eye from the pastoral scene.

"Where've you been?" our new friend asked conversationally, while we walked.

"Oh, we've just had the best visit to Chartwell. Such an elegant home and such fascinating history from the room guides."

"Oh right, yes, she's a beauty all right. And did they tell you about some of Winnie's famous quotes?" He started chuckling to himself.

"No. Steve, did anyone tell you about Churchill's famous quotes?" I asked, turning towards him.

"Nope. No one said anything to me." Steve was too busy trying to get a perfect photo of the outstanding view with Archie and Millie rooting in the grasses around him, to get involved in our chit-chat.

"Right," said the gentleman, "I'll tell you one that is very famous but not very flattering about Mr Churchill. The story goes that the Prime Minister had imbibed one too many alcoholic beverages, you see, and was being rather aggressive and rude. A woman at the dinner party said to him rather haughtily, 'I'd kill myself if I was married to you.' To which Churchill replied, 'Madam, if you were married to me, I would have saved you the trouble and done it for you!'"

"That's actually very good," I snorted, laughing. But the next one was incredibly rude too. Churchill was very drunk (again) and yet another snooty woman pointed out this fact to him, saying, 'Winston, you are drunk, horribly drunk.' His slurred reply was: 'And you, madam, are ugly, horribly ugly – but I shall be sober tomorrow.'

Churchill was certainly very quick-witted, but I don't think I'd have enjoyed being on the end of his often-acerbic wit.

Back at the village green we said farewell to our companion and his two dogs and plonked ourselves down in the bus shelter, waiting to retrace our steps home. I closed my eyes for a few minutes, listening to the birds in the trees and the background drone of a lawnmower. My reverie was rudely interrupted by Steve's elbow in my ribs. "Oy, wake up. The bus is coming. Remember we're stopping in Brixton on the way home?"

It took me a minute to remember why we were stopping in

Brixton. "Oh yes, the wine tasting." I was feeling quite sleepy and really, I would have preferred just to go straight home but the New Zealand Wine Cellar was having a *free* sauvignon blanc tasting. It was going to be 'help yourself' so it would be rude not to turn up! So many of the country's big, as well as boutique, vineyards would be represented.

It was standing room only at the Brixton store and what a buzzy atmosphere, on a very hot and still London evening. A cacophony of New Zealand accents bubbled over the squeeze of people crowded into the square. After a raucous hour and a half, chatting with all and sundry, meeting loads of London Kiwis and sampling way too many sauvignon blancs, it was time to go. I managed to push my way gently over to Steve, who was totally engaged and well settled in with a bunch of blokes and tap him on the shoulder. "It's time to go!" I yelled over the racket.

Steve just pulled a face at me, turned back to his new best friends, muttered something I couldn't hear and reluctantly drained his glass. I know he would have liked to stay, but any longer and he would have had to carry me out. It had all been too tempting.

Before I continue, I should clarify who the Richards are. There's Bridget and Richard – friends in Gretton, Anne and Richard – who own the B&B around the corner and Richard – who lived across the hallway in our flats.

It was almost three months since we'd arrived. Slowly, bearing in mind the usual English reserve coming into play, we were getting to know our flatmates. Of course, people said hello when passing on the stairs, in the driveway or up the High Street, and Richard who lived at No. 10 and Terry at No. 11 had polite but brief chats outside our doors, but no one else had. I'd passed one of the two men from one of the bottom flats a few times in the mornings in the High Street and always said hello. This morning he stopped.

"You often catch me in my track pants at this time of day, so I thought I should explain. In case you thought I was a bit of a slob," he said sheepishly.

I must have mumbled something like "I hadn't noticed." I really hadn't, but then he went on to say, "I go swimming most mornings at the leisure centre," pointing up the street, "and it's easy to pull these on to go home in and have a shower there."

"Perfectly sensible and acceptable," I smiled at him. "I'm Annemarie." I extended my hand which he took, shaking it heartily.

"And I'm Stephen. Big Stephen, from the bottom flat. Little Stephen is my partner."

"Well, I'm not likely to forget your names. My husband is Stephen too." We both laughed.

"You're obviously the Kiwis the others were talking about. You're certainly not English as I've noticed you're always in bright colours or florals."

"We most certainly are," I grinned at him. "We're in Ken and Irene's flat, next to Terry and opposite Richard."

"Yes, Richard said he'd met you and chatted already. Well, it's very nice to meet you. I'm sure this won't be the last time you find me in the High Street in my track pants." Again, we laughed and parted company.

That was the beginning of a special friendship with the two Stephens. Big Stephen was a top sales rep for Arran, a Scottish fragrance company and Little Stephen, a fabulous florist at the charming Bramble & Moss Flowers in Richmond. While we lived in Teddington, we had some special and great times with them, and with Richard.

I just love the train and it's the easiest way to get to Bridget and Richard in the village of Gretton, travelling from St Pancras International to Corby in the East Midlands. The weekend had been planned to within an inch of its life – food and wine, participants, entertainment and touring. We'd been looking forward to this long weekend, knowing it would be good fun and interesting. We weren't disappointed.

We'd no sooner dropped our bags in the upstairs bedroom, downed a sandwich and a cup of tea before we were hustled out the door. The beautiful, timeless town of Stamford beckoned for a delightful potter in and around the boutiques and a peaceful meander beside the River Welland. Not that it's ever peaceful when Bridget and I get together. Steve and Richard do lots of nodding and eye-rolling, finding it quite difficult to get a word in edgeways. I should stress that Bridget and my conversations are always very interesting and intellectual ... to us.

Bridget checked her watch. "Richard, it's just on three o'clock. It's terribly thirsty work all this window shopping, walking and talking. Why don't we see if there's a free table at The George? Have afternoon tea there. Steve," Bridget tapped him on the arm, "do you fancy a cream tea? A scone with jam and delicious English clotted cream?"

In my book *My French Platter*, I'd made it known that Steve was always starving. He'd already leapt ten steps ahead of us and pushed the door to The George open, when he suddenly remembered us and glanced back. "Are you lot coming then? Hurry up. We don't want to miss out on a table!"

Bridget struggled to stifle a snort, Richard smirked at me, and I apologised to them both. "So sorry! He's got dreadful manners. You'd think he hadn't eaten for a week. Honestly. Let's hope he's secured a table."

I can truly vouch for The George's beautifully crafted and light scones, smothered in the purest, most unctuous clotted cream and topped with a very fruity raspberry jam, tasting of summer. This hotel would be one of the most ancient (and elegant) in all of England. There's many a floral, upholstered, and cushioned nook and cranny where 'one' can sit to partake of a cream tea, as well as a little tipple of champagne.

The ornate and gloriously turned staircase and dark wood panelling throughout is original and the restaurant has a most enviable reputation. I should imagine staying at The George is a luxury 'one' needs to indulge in, but not this 'one'. We had our own little bit of luxury staying with Bridget and Richard, even though it's dangerous. Why? I'll explain in a minute.

Luckily there was 'me time' factored into our hectic weekend itinerary and, once home, I slipped away to our bedroom for a little lie down and a quiet read. Suddenly, I was being shaken. Steve was standing there and stooped to pick my book up off the floor. "Rattle yourself, sleeping beauty. We're off again. Get your lipstick and shoes on."

I took a minute to gather myself and prop up on my elbows. "Where to? Where are we going? I thought we were going to help with dinner?"

"Too late. 'Her indoors' has already gone and done it. All sorted. We're going to the pub. C'mon."

Lipstick and shoes on, a quick brush of the hair, I assembled myself at the bottom of the stairs, heading for the back door, ready to jump in the car.

"Where do you think you're going, missus?" Richard hollered from somewhere in the house. "We're waiting for you – at the front door. We're walking."

Fifty paces from their front door was the pub – that's why it's dangerous. Walk down their path, out the gate, across the road and straight in through the Blue Bell's front door. Way too close for sobriety. It's very handy though, just to bung something in the oven, trot over for a drink and pop home mid-glass, to check on dinner. Introductions made, the locals were so welcoming. We spent a very convivial hour (and more) in this newly renovated little pub, full of historic charm, but with a modern twist. If it wasn't for the pretty blue iron signboard swinging above the doorway, you'd think you were walking into someone's front room. The exterior looks just like one of the old stone homes in the village.

As you can imagine, dinner was a little late that night, but Bridget's beautiful, stuffed sea bass, steamed asparagus and salad on the side was devoured with great relish – when it eventually reached the table. Everything she created was a work of art and so full of flavour. The fish was stripped down to its bones, with a lot of false bravado about who was going to eat the eye ... I swear it winked at me when I scraped it into the bin, before loading the dishwasher. Okay, maybe I'd had one too many wines by that stage.

Saturday dawned fine and clear, and we arrived in the kitchen to find an exquisitely set breakfast table, laden with cereals, fruit, juices, a choice of toast and spreads, tea and coffee and 'would we like eggs and bacon too?' I'm so glad we chose to stay with Bridget and Richard. The accommodation and service were far superior to The George.

With the dishwasher stacked and the table cleared, we grabbed jackets and bags and waddled out to the car. Well, it felt as though we waddled, after such an amazing breakfast. Richard's steady hands on the wheel guided us to our first stop at Oakham Castle.

To my eye, the architecture was quite plain and nothing like a 'usual' castle, with crenellated walls and towers. This one was Norman, and the Great Hall is apparently the finest surviving example of Norman architecture in Europe, built between 1180 and 1190. The Great Hall is famed for its unique collection of over 230 ornate ceremonial horseshoes donated by peers of the realm (royalty and nobility such as dukes, marquesses, earls, viscounts, barons and bishops). The oldest surviving horseshoe was given to the castle by Edward IV in 1470 and every one of the horseshoes has a story. Don't worry, I'm not going to recount each story.

Don't you just love all this history, though? New Zealanders struggle to get to grips with just how old the UK and Europe are. We have nothing like it.

Steve and Richard went off for 18 holes of golf during the afternoon and Bridget and I gave our voices a rest – at least until it was time to head out for dinner at The George and Dragon in another pretty village called Seaton. These English country pubs are so divine, and this was another where there was a sense of being in someone's home. Everyone chats to everyone else, and the locals and staff make newcomers feel like part of a family. I love it and fully immerse myself when I can. This inviting two-roomed bistro pub featured bare brick walls and tweed upholstery and had a cosy bar with a roaring fire on one side and a simply fitted-out restaurant on the other, serving the best home-cooked meals. With plenty of choice Steve homed in on the beer-battered haddock while I went for the slow-roasted lamb shoulder. Always, always there's a side of fries.

The Sunday breakfast service at Bridget and Richard's was just as good as Saturday's so I think Steve and I will be booking in again. Burghley House and Gardens was our first stop that day. If the name rings a bell, it's because of the Burghley Horse Trials, which are held there every year. This glorious house was designed and built by William Cecil, the 1st Lord Burghley (1520–98), Lord High Treasurer and Chief Minister to Queen Elizabeth I. The house was inherited by his descendants, the Earls and Marquesses of Exeter, until the death of the 6th

Marquess as recently as 1981, when the house and its contents became part of a charitable trust. The title was inherited by the Marquess' brother and is currently held by his nephew, Michael, 8th Marquess of Exeter.

Today, the Burghley House Preservation Trust administers the property, in which there has been an extensive and ongoing programme of conservation and restoration work for the last three decades. Burghley is still lived in by a direct descendant of William Cecil, Miranda Rock, together with her husband Orlando and their four children.

While we were visiting, Miranda Rock was wandering around chatting to visitors. Imagine being able to trace your ancestry back to the sixteenth century. Mind-boggling. The rooms were so ornate and beautiful, packed with centuries-old treasures of furniture, art, ornaments, tapestries and carpets. My favourite room was the original Elizabethan kitchen – gleaming copper pots, terrines, jelly moulds and oven baking dishes. About 250 of them were displayed on shelves and walls around the interior. It was the biggest kitchen I'd ever seen, and the original fireplaces now contain ranges and modern appliances.

A sculpture exhibition was on in the magnificent grounds and, after a cuppa in the House tea rooms, we whiled away a few hours exploring these and the expansive garden. Last stop before home was a drink at another favourite inn – Jackson Stops, a very pretty, Grade II listed 'chocolate box' thatched roof cottage, set back from the road. Here, there were four separate dining rooms that apparently had roaring fires blazing in the winter and a garden to eat in during the hot summer days.

No weekend at Bridget and Richard's is complete without them hosting a delectable dinner and this Sunday night Bridget cooked for seven of us. I didn't let her do all of it single-handed, but she and Richard had a great system going, moving easily around each other in the kitchen – he washes up and puts away as Bridget is finished with things. I *did* try to help but got told off, in no uncertain terms. "Annemarie, would you sit down! You're crowding the kitchen," Bridget muttered, pushing past me to get to the hob.

"Annemarie, would you sit down! And stop using the hand towel to dry the dishes," Richard tutted, snatching the towel from me. It was all said with great humour and silly grins but I *was* only trying to help!

"If you want to earn your keep and help, here, pod these." Bridget thrust a bowl of broad beans into my hands, placing an empty bowl on the table for the skins. Trust me to get that job. It takes forever, but they really do need to be podded to savour their sweetness.

It was such a fun night, and once the dinner debris had been cleared, the playing cards came out. Too many wines were imbibed to make much sense of contract whist and the evening deteriorated into raucous hilarity with the cards thrown into the air, the chairs pushed back, and the music turned up. I wonder who did that? Wild dancing ensued, arms draped over shoulders and hips twisted across the kitchen floor. Booker T and the MGs belted out 'Green Onions' and we rocked and grooved until the wee hours. I'd no idea what time everyone left, but we crawled into bed at some silly hour.

No, I didn't have a headache on Sunday morning and there was no time to get self-indulgent if I did. We needed to fit in a trip to Foxton Locks before our mid-afternoon train back to London.

What a fascinating place the Locks was, watching them in action with the narrow boats lined up ready to go through each one, set in two staircases, down the hillside. It takes about 45 minutes for a boat to go through all the locks – a marvellous piece of engineering and created in such a beautiful countryside setting.

Sadly, it was time to go. I'd need a few days to recover from all that fabulous food, wine and touring. On the train, staring into vacant space as the view rushed past, I'd felt rather flat. It had been a busy and fun-filled time with Bridget and Richard. They felt more like family than friends.

May Snippets

Osterley Park and House, one of the last surviving country estates in Hounslow, London. It sits right in the middle of suburbia but, when built, would have definitely been in the country. Even with all the surrounding houses, Osterley retains a country house and park ambiance. Renovated in the late eighteenth century by architect and designer, Robert Adam, for the extremely wealthy Child family as a residence in which to entertain and impress their friends and clients, Osterley is presented as it would have looked in the 1780s. The interior was all Robert's work as well, done in a stunning neo-classical style with ornate panelling and cornices. The guided tour telling about the creation of the house and the families that had lived there was brilliant.

Sky Garden, Fenchurch Street, in the heart of the city, is free, but make sure to book a timeslot online before coming to London. The views, city architecture and other rooftop gardens are spectacular even on an overcast day. I think it's a must-do.

Royalty. London had the hottest May Bank Holiday since records began: 27 °C. It was almost too hot to be out on the London streets. Everywhere, excitement was building and the hype was palpable for the wedding of Meghan and Harry, to the point where a friend of ours who lives in Windsor had moved out until the wedding was over, saying it was already so difficult to move around the town, hectic with excitable tourists and busy cafés and restaurants.

In our village of Teddington patriotic flags were flying from every building in the High Street and the hanging flower baskets were replenished with vibrant, colourful petunias cascading over the sides. Early morning walks up the High Street saw us crossing the road to avoid a drenching from the dedicated men on the back of trucks watering all these flowers from the tanks.

The shops were full of royal family wedding 'merchandise', the hottest being the masks of all the family members, Union Jack cupcake holders, mini flags attached to skewers and three-tier cupcake stands. It was all so cheap at £1 per item and a young woman, with her arms full of all the paraphernalia available, stepped out of the Teddington Essentials store, telling me the pub she worked at was hosting a royal wedding afternoon tea. It would be just one of many on the day, I was sure.

I'd stupidly booked a play, *The Book of Mormon*, on the royal wedding day so only saw some of the wedding on TV. Piccadilly Circus was crazy with royalists, and pubs were overflowing with exuberant fans. Everywhere people were singing, wearing royal face masks, waving flags and spilling out of garden bars. It was hard to move along the pavement to get to the theatre, but it was fun to be part of the wedding hype for a brief time.

After a busy day, we escaped the heat of the flat, going through the gate in the fence into the park next door and enjoyed a cool drink beside the river. Dinner would have to wait. It was just too hot to be cooking.

Instead of using the fence gate, Steve and I strolled back along the short path beside the water which pops out beside The Anglers pub. The garden bar was heaving with families; others were walking and cycling, crossing the Lock Bridge for a stroll or a ride along the Thames Path. Summer was on the way.

The following link will take you directly to photos associated with May. Feel free to comment on any of them.

https://bit.ly/LLA_May-2018

JUNE 2018
KEW GARDENS; V&A EXHIBITIONS;
PEZENAS, FRANCE

With Steve's tremendous help, I finished the basement flat project in Shepherd's Bush. It was unrecognisable as the smelly, damp, neglected and bare space that first greeted me; it now presented as a welcoming and inviting space to live in.

The damp wall in the hall was treated, painters redecorated where necessary, new shelving was constructed in the living area and bedroom, and curtains and sofa covers dry-cleaned. I replaced all the bed linen and pillows. Steve pulled out the bed and armoire from the walls and cleaned down and vacuumed behind everything and around ceiling cornices. He was brilliant at getting stuck into the cupboard under the stairs where too many spiders, cobwebs and creepy things lived, and the outdoor cupboard in the little backyard area (more spiders, cobwebs and creepy things). The outdoor pavers had come up a treat once Steve scrubbed off all the deep mould and dug up roots and weeds between them. The front steps and the butanol top of the bin cupboards were looking pristine too.

The original sofa, TV and cabinet, coffee table and small dining table and chairs were staying so I needed to work around these and improve the look. I'd spent hours on the

Internet searching for appropriate items. IKEA, H&M and M&S proved fruitful with some purchases, but I splashed out on quality mirrors, a canvas, and nice prints – all with the owner's prior approval, of course. I bought 90 per cent of the items online and had them delivered to our flat where everything could be safely stored in our dry garage. It would all be sold with the flat. Once everything arrived, I booked a man and a van for a Saturday morning and, with everything loaded, Steve and I jumped in the front seat with the driver, tootling our way through to Shepherd's Bush to unload and set up at the flat.

The last item installed was a DVS-type system, after waiting seven weeks to get the installers there. The air is constantly re-circulated throughout the flat and creates a dry living environment without condensation or mould. Irene and Ken had one installed in the flat we were in and what a difference it made.

The flat looked and smelt so good, giving a potential buyer a glimpse of the home it could be. I was very proud of it. The estate agents arrived and took professional photos creating good interest, with one buyer very keen. Buying and selling property in England could be a long, protracted process, so it was a waiting game.

By June we'd spent quite a bit of time with Anne and Richard. Richard and Steve were now regularly meeting up with a great bunch of guys at the Builders Arms for a convivial beer, a lot of sparring and fixing world politics – all before dinner! So at least once a week, Steve was getting a little respite from me and enjoying the company of men.

"Are you keeping busy, while you wait for your exam results?" Richard had asked him, while they chatted companionably over a beer. "I must say, having to wait three months seems a bit ridiculous."

"Absolutely ridiculous. Couldn't agree more. No one told us it would take that long, until after the exams were over. Annemarie and I were shocked, to be honest." Steve fiddled with his beer mat, feeling a bit aggrieved at having to wait so long. "There's plenty to see and do, of course, but, in the meantime, I wouldn't mind earning a bit of money. I'm open to anything really. I enjoy mowing lawns and doing general garden and outdoor work. That sort of thing."

"Right, well I'll keep my ears open, and I'll mention it to Anne. We'll let you know if we hear of anything going. I'll get the other half in before we head home for supper. My turn." Richard collected up their empty half pints and inched his way through to the bar.

When Steve came in from the pub that night and told me about his conversation with Richard, we got talking about what our next steps might be. It was now June. Delayed exam results, the tight restrictions for the fire risk assessment jobs and the required experience were making it extremely difficult for Steve to get a foot in the door. He'd basically come to a dead end with our friend's colleague and after 30 years in the fire risk assessment business, he himself was struggling with all the new regulations and having to retrain in some areas. That door was now firmly closed.

After investing all that time and money into the risk assessment courses, Steve still wanted to pursue roles in that field, but would also investigate other areas while waiting to see what his exam results were. We were now into our fourth month of not earning much and, each month, I was transferring a large sum of money from our savings in New Zealand to our NatWest account in London, to cover rent, council tax, insurances, out-of-town travel and food. Thank goodness local travel (in the London zones) was free for us. For every New Zealand dollar I transferred, we received 50 British pence. So, as an example, if I transferred NZ$1,000 we received £500. We were literally 'watching our pennies'.

I was being frugal and would pack our lunch for a day out, treating ourselves to coffee or a glass of wine somewhere. Aldi made a superb replica of the French *pain aux raisins* every day, so I'd freeze some as soon as I got home from shopping, and we'd take one of these with us.

The morning after Steve and Richard's chat my phone rang. It was Anne. "Morning! As you know, we're booked to go away next week. Richard was telling me that Steve's up for some garden work. How would he feel about clearing out our garden shed? The compost heap needs a good tidy up too. It seems to have spread itself too far. Of course, we'd be paying him. Please, just say if he's not keen. I'd totally understand. Not everyone likes doing that sort of thing."

"I think he'd be up for that but let me have a chat with him and I'll ring you back. Thanks Anne."

Steve was perfectly happy to do the job and, when he went around to see exactly what needed doing, Anne had a quiet word in his ear. "I'd be so grateful, Steve. Richard's never going to get around to it while he's working, and it bugs me what a mess it's in. We're both guilty of flinging the tools in there and just pulling the door shut on it. Then, when I go back, I can never find anything."

Arrangements made, Anne and Richard went off on holiday. Steve got stuck in. By the time he'd finished you could see your reflection in the spade and shovel and all tools were hung like soldiers standing to attention, everything in size order along the back wall. Small tools, garden twine, hooks and bits and bobs were all allocated to a box or basket and the mouldy, muck-caked terracotta pots were washed, dried in the sun and stacked in appropriate sizes, ready for re-planting when Anne so desired. The lawn mower was cleaned down, the walls brushed clean, and the potting bench swept and readied for work. No spider dared climb inside that shed again. Webs had been removed and the floor swept of long-dead creepy-crawlies.

Anne's text message on her return was full of exclamation marks, and cries of joy would have been heard if she'd recorded her message, so delighted was she with the result of all Steve's hard work. The word went out and Steve began work for one of their neighbours.

After appreciating what Steve had achieved at her place, Anne decided we needed to get ourselves registered on a website called Next Door, which is the same as Neighbourly, back in New Zealand. I duly drafted up an appropriate blurb for the site, introducing and selling ourselves as project managers, cleaners, gardener, home stagers, cook and administrator and uploaded it. We were inundated. The messages tumbled in, one after the other.

That night, a woman who runs a downsizing/de-cluttering business got in touch and we met for coffee. Steve was immediately recruited for two major projects and the following month I joined her for de-cluttering and assisting with her admin work.

The requests for our cleaning services came thick and fast. After a little juggling and being fussy about for whom and where I worked, I settled into a Tuesday–Thursday rota. This left me with Monday and Friday and the weekend, as my days to do as I pleased. Along with the need to earn some money, we wanted to balance it with having time to get out and do things – and to travel a little. So, officially, I became a cleaner, a de-clutterer and an administrator.

I decided to go cleaning for two reasons. One, my rate was a better hourly rate than I'd receive in an office or medical practice. Two, it gave me great flexibility. I was able to say, 'I'm away for the week of ...' or 'I can't do Thursday, the 30th, but I could swap to the Friday.' I couldn't do that in an office role. I settled on three clients, and all were very amenable, very nice and with lovely homes. I couldn't bear to clean a dirty home ... The best thing was it was only for three hours at a time. I could walk home, shower and be off into London in the afternoon or meeting up with people locally.

One 'client' couple was Anne and Bruce and once we'd agreed that I was available at a time and date suitable to both parties, I was summoned for an interview with Bruce and asked to bring my passport to verify my identity. That was a first for me. Anne had an appointment and was unable to be there.

"You must be Annemarie. I'm Bruce. Do come in." Bruce held the door wide, and I walked down a short hallway and into a modern, light and airy kitchen. Sun was streaming in through the French doors which opened out into a longish, narrow and beautifully kept garden.

"This is lovely, Bruce. What a nice place you have," I said, admiring the kitchen and garden.

"Yes, these townhouses are very nice and we're in such a handy location – for both Teddington and Kingston. Please, have a seat. Can I get you a coffee?"

"Oh yes please. Lovely." I sat down at the dining table, pulled my passport out of my bag and pushed it across the table to where I could see he'd be sitting. A perfectly aligned notepad and pens and glass of water sat ready and waiting for the interview process to begin.

Bruce was tall, nicely dressed in an open neck shirt and chinos and wearing a pair of casual slip-on shoes. He was pleasant looking, wearing frameless glasses and sporting a well-clipped moustache. His short salt and pepper hair was neatly groomed.

It came as no surprise when Bruce announced that he was ex-military. The giveaways were the moustache, the precision setting of the stationery, the need to view my passport and undergo an interview – for a cleaner's job ...

Bruce and I got on well and after a great chat and him showing me through the three floors of the house, he escorted me to the front door. "I've got a feeling this arrangement is going to be dangerous," he said sternly, as he opened the door.

"Oh?" I was a bit taken aback and looked up at him.

"Yes, I can see you and my wife are going to get on very well," he laughed. "Why don't we all meet for a coffee soon, in the Fallow Deer in the High Street? Anne can then meet you and give you the seal of approval. Not that I think there'll be an issue. Bring Steve with you. I'll get Anne to send a message and you two can set a time."

We did have that meet up and yes, we did all get on well. From then on and each time I went to clean, we'd have a coffee and a chat together first, then Anne and Bruce would disappear for the morning, and I'd get on with the job. They were great people and as time went on, we four became good friends.

Kew Botanical Gardens, in Southwest London, is a magnificent place, home to 300 acres of botanical gardens with 50,000 species, along with the Palm House and the Temperate House. The Palm House is one of the first buildings ever constructed using wrought iron and it's extraordinary to be inside and up close to see how the iron connects and the glass is fitted. Almost-extinct species from around the world co-exist here and it was incredibly hot and steamy. As is to be expected, the Temperate House has a more comfortable climate and is the largest surviving glasshouse in the world. It was gleaming when we visited, having undergone major restoration.

The many different gardens at Kew gave off the most heavenly scents and the plants, trees and wide-open spaces created such a stunning and tranquil setting. That was until we sat down in the Japanese Zen Garden where I timed aircraft coming into land at Heathrow every 90 seconds ... Not terribly 'zen' like at all!

Many people, like us, had packed lunch and sprawled themselves on the lawn or were seated on one of the many benches dotted around the park. Kew Palace, set at one end of the gardens, is very modest but must be visited. It was called the Dutch House before being renamed as Kew Palace (once royalty arrived) and it is distinctive in its architecture and red-brick colour. The kitchen garden was a celebration of flourishing herbs and vegetables of every kind, all of which was used in the café and on-site restaurant. The enormous, espaliered fig tree planted in 1975 was like a triffid, with its tentacle-like branches reaching upwards and outwards. It wouldn't be long before it was heavy with pendulous figs.

The Waterlily House was specifically designed to showcase the giant, vividly lime-green Amazon water lilies which have huge circular leaves and upturned rims. They can reach up to 10 feet wide and supposedly take the weight of a small child. Incredible. To me, these lilies looked like edible spinach flans, floating on the pond.

Steve and I stopped for coffee in Kew village and at the back of the café was a rustic, wooden sign, hanging on a wall (see photograph). In other words – supervise your children and don't let them run wild! I loved it.

Late June, and after a 2.30 a.m. start in London, friends Gin and Dave collected us from Montpellier airport, whisking us through to Nîmes for a strong coffee to keep us going. Coming up from a car park, we watched a stunning white carriage with black wheels and ornate, black side lamps being pulled by two very tall, glossy black horses parading an elegant bride and groom through the streets. They were on their way to the local *Mairie*, to be married. The horses stood patiently waiting for the bollards to descend underground so they could pass through.

After a stroll through the old town, admiring the Roman amphitheatre, we ended up at a sumptuous indoor market. Ginny and I were in heaven. The fruit and vegetable selections were outstanding – vibrant-red beefsteak tomatoes, deep-burgundy heirloom ones, fat, juicy green bundles of asparagus, unblemished white fennel with frothy green fronds, glossy black and pendulous aubergines, were all neatly aligned and displayed to perfection.

"It's time for lunch," Ginny declared coming out of the market, "all that amazing food has got me salivating." There was no argument from us.

A little family-run restaurant had an inviting menu posted in the window and many locals inside. That was always a good sign. We four squashed around one of the last tables available and dived into a delicious and generous lunch with a bottle of rosé for the girls and beers for the boys. Steve found Heineken, with a distinctive Māori label emblazoned with *Nouvelle-Zelande* on the drinks list and had to have it. With full bellies we toddled out of the restaurant and into a vivid blue sky and warm day. Nîmes was showing us just how stunning she was with her wide boulevards, lush gardens, sparkling and ornate fountains and an interesting waterfall running through the pedestrian walkway on Ave. Feucheres. I was so happy to be back in my much-adored France.

Late in the afternoon Dave dropped us at the door of our B&B in Pezenas. "You'll be perfectly safe here. Gin and I wandered up yesterday to see where you would be staying and noticed there's a doctor two doors down, the *Mairie* four doors down and the police station at the end of the road," he chuckled.

Our room, up two flights of stairs, was long and narrow, beautifully clean, containing all that we needed with a bonus view over our cobbled street. I could sit on the little balcony with my early cup of tea and watch the world go by beneath me. A cat, sunning itself and having a lazy wash on the window ledge opposite, was doing exactly that.

Pezenas, in the department of Herault, is a small town of about 9,000 people, located between Béziers and Montpellier and only 20 minutes from the Mediterranean. The well-preserved historic, pedestrianised centre with many picturesque streets to wander in is a joy. The town is full of artists' studios, *brocantes* and many independent boutiques.

Dave and Gin were staying with their extended family in a beautifully furnished old villa on the edge of town, with a large stone patio and a pool, plenty big enough for those wanting to get some exercise and do lengths. Steve and I shared food and wine with the group, arriving after breakfast, sometimes bringing heavenly French pastries and leaving as the sun was setting around 10.00 p.m. It's just too hard to pass a true French patisserie and not stop to buy a *mille-feuille, pain aux raisins*, a raspberry tart or some pastry oozing with *crème pâtissier* and a light dusting of icing sugar. *Ooh la la!* So delightful.

Always after dinner, we felt compelled to go wandering in the still-warm evenings through the back alleyways and streets, looking up at many coloured and varied iron balconies and the homes of the locals. Everywhere we looked, striking, cerise-pink and purple bougainvillea vines trailed under windows and over doorways. One heavily laden bough hung low over a royal-blue door, creating a riot of colour against the old stone building. A gentle stroll back to fall into the 28 °C pool just before we headed home to bed was absolute heaven.

In Pezenas, every Wednesday in July and August from 7.30 p.m. onwards music, wine and food evenings are held and people can sit at the trestle tables set out in the pedestrian centre. Delectable aromas fill the air from the various food stalls, and locals and tourists mingle, sharing fabulous food, wine, and great conversation. Live music plays and children flit from table to table, gathering their friends up to dance or to play tag in any spare space. These are fabulous evenings that continue through to sunset.

No visit to France is complete without spending time at one of the many food markets, choosing succulent delicacies for lunch and dinner. Always there are several cheeses as well as the daily golden-brown crusted baguettes. Juicy red, ripe tomatoes that taste of childhood are carefully selected and popped into the basket, alongside crisp, curly green lettuces, vivid-red capsicums and snap-worthy beans.

Our sightseeing during that relaxing week included the Fonseranes Locks, a flight of staircase locks near Béziers on the famous Canal du Midi, having lunch in Béziers itself where the lovely French couple departing the table next to us kindly handed us their unfinished bottle of wine. The Saint Nazaire Cathedral in Béziers was another beauty discovered, as was the collegiate church of Saint-Etienne in Capestang. St David (Ginny's Dave) bought an English newspaper and a beer and was happily ensconced in a chair catching up on British news and the football results, waiting patiently for us to return from our wanderings.

Dave drove us all over the Herault region and a special day was spent at Abbaye de Valmagne, a former monastery founded in 1139 and one of the most beautiful and richest Cistercian abbeys in France. It's also home to one of the oldest vineyards in the Languedoc. The wine is for sale and there's also accommodation available at the abbey. The fireplaces were cavernous, and Steve could easily stand inside one. Stone seating had been built inside but I wasn't sure whether people did actually sit in there. There was easily room to spit-roast a whole beast.

On we drove to Bouzigues to have the most succulent lunch beside the sea. Mine was a plate of fat, sweet, juicy orange *crevettes* (prawns), the others having *moules et frites* (mussels and fries). A vast number of oysters and mussel farms, their produce growing in the sparkling azure sea, were just offshore.

During our last day touring, we came across a beautiful monument at Pierrerue, near Capestang. It was on this spot that resistance fighters from the region were murdered by the Nazis, and each man and woman had been named and recorded. It was a very sobering moment. We took the time to think of them, so grateful none of us ever had to endure the horrors of war.

Our week had flown by – out touring early in the cool, fresh morning air, having coffee in an ancient village square with a water fountain tinkling nearby before exploring the area, then a little lunch and home again to lie in the shade around the pool to read, or doze during the soporific heat of the afternoon, or, for the more active, to take a cooling swim. It was the perfect holiday.

Our last morning, which we'd planned to spend at the huge Saturday market in the square, was totally ruined by the news that our flight back to London from Montpellier had been cancelled because of the French air traffic controllers' strike. Nothing was available from any of the nearby airports for four days. I was so stressed by it.

However, the cancellation turned into a bonus when Dave

suggested we take the train to Toulouse and stay with old friends Siobhan and Doug, who'd taken us in when we were sacked from Mas de Lavande (as recounted in *My French Platter*), out near Gaillac. We'd then fly from Toulouse to Luton airport – which meant not getting back to Teddington until 12.45 a.m. on Tuesday morning and running out the door again at 7.45 a.m. to catch a train to Cambridge for the day. Aargh!

June Snippets

Dangerous liaisons. As Bruce predicted, we *were* on dangerous ground. I met up with his wife Anne to have coffee and a walk. Later that week I cleaned her house. I could see it was going to be one of those 'crossing a fine line' situations, as employee/employer. I felt confident we'd work it out, as Mary and I did, and Anne and I got on well. She asked me to be part of a new book club – a group of five – which she thought would introduce me to yet more women with their own stories and backgrounds. I was looking forward to it.

Elderflower trees were everywhere and in full bloom. Their fragrance was very distinctive and intoxicating. Bridget had made elderflower cordial and I decided to give it a go, using Jamie Oliver's recipe. I left it to steep for a couple of days, giving it a stir now and then. The heady perfume filled our flat! So much sugar in it, but the recipe is one part cordial, four parts soda/sparkling water/prosecco – I liked the sound of the third option best. Or the cordial could be used to flavour cake icing, giving it the most delicate flavour.

Victoria and Albert Museum exhibitions. An impromptu lunch with friend Mary at the new V&A members' dining room and a special visit to the Frida Kahlo exhibition. It was brilliant and such an insight into her life, art, family and political leanings. An extremely difficult life but faced with great fortitude. Frida's clothes were so traditionally Mexican.

Fashioned from Nature Exhibition. So good. Some of the clothing dating from the seventeenth century was just exquisite, showing what was made from ivory, bamboo, flax, feathers, cotton and oil and what clothing came from nature, caused pollution and the near extinction of some birds – some examples being that the cotton factories created pollution and illness; feathers used meant some birds were hunted nearly to extinction.

On display were the funkiest pair of crocheted trousers — 'peggy squares' in vivid yellow, green, pink, red and black, all stitched together. It just showed what could be done with leftover yarn ... Anything goes here in London so I could easily visualise someone wearing the crochet trousers. On my last visit to the Royal Academy with Mary we watched a dark and handsome, bearded man with a very hairy chest and wearing an exquisite halter-neck dress and heels, saunter down the steps towards us. See what I mean?

Take a June moment. Right then, in the middle of June, I was living in the moment and loving life, finding happiness and joy in the smallest things. Most days brought new experiences and very nice people along the way. The notion that the British were standoffish was ridiculous. Neither Steve nor I experienced it. Mind you, New Zealand doesn't have a class system and most New Zealanders feel that we fit in with people from all walks of life. So the British can't put us in a box of which school we went to, who our parents were and what suburb we live in!

I was having wonderful encounters on buses, trains and in the supermarkets with people young and old from all over the world. Life felt good.

The following link will take you directly to photos associated with June. Feel free to comment on any of them.

https://bit.ly/LLA_June-2018

JULY 2018
CAMBRIDGE, HAMPTON COURT FLOWER SHOW; PRINCESS DIANA EXHIBITION; SCOTLAND

This was such a cultural and people-packed month, it felt as if our feet hardly touched the ground.

"What time does your train get into Cambridge?" Barb was on the phone.

"I think we arrive about 10 a.m. We want to make a day of it and see as much as possible before we meet up with you," I replied.

"Oh, you absolutely must. It's a great city to explore. See you at dinner. Nessie and Allan are looking forward to seeing you both. Must fly, Annemarie. Gemma says we need to be downstairs in five minutes and I haven't put my face on yet!"

Barb was over from New Zealand catching up with family in London and cousins and aunt and uncle, Nessie and Allan, in Glasgow. Barb was born in Glasgow and had come to New Zealand with her parents at the age of 11. Steve and I had spent time with Nessie and Allan often, when they came to Auckland to stay with Barb and Gerard, for a month at a time. I could sit and listen to their Scottish voices all day, with the odd questioning look at Barb and asking, "What did he say?" Uncle Allan has a strong Glaswegian accent and, at times, an unintelligible one to me! But they are the loveliest people. Barb had brought them to Cambridge to see the sights and to catch up with their great-niece, Gemma, Barb's daughter. Gemma was studying, extramurally from New Zealand, to complete a two-year Masters' Degree in Property. Every three months, she would fly into London and catch the train to Cambridge for two weeks to attend live-in course work, staying in the student halls.

Bleary-eyed, we'd stepped off the train at Cambridge into a blazing hot sun and a throng of people. It was bustling and buzzing with tourists, university students and their families. Tour guides, with their flags raised high, were shadowed by an ant trail of people, taking in their every word, via an earpiece.

Cambridge has been described as the only true university town in England as the university and colleges provide nearly all the historical architectural features. Our heads were swivelling, taking it all in, walking through as many colleges as we could, loving the beauty not only of the buildings but also the green common areas.

Reclining in our punt on the river Cam and gliding past all the colleges, our punter was one of the many college students employed over their summer break to take tourists like us out for an hour. Ours gave us chapter-and-verse on the history of each of the colleges whilst deftly navigating the punt through the *mélange* of many others on the river, trying to avoid a collision. The banter between the punting students was witty and amusing.

"Och, Annemarie, it's so lovely to see you!" Aunt Nessie exclaimed when we rushed through the restaurant door. I stooped to put my arms around this lovely Scottish woman, who must've stood less than five feet tall in her stockinged feet. I smiled to myself, enjoying her lilting accent.

"And you, Aunt Nessie, don't look a day older than when I last saw you." She and Uncle Allan were always full of life and always smiling. I'd have loved them to be my aunt and uncle.

After a superb dinner, endless chit-chat, and several glasses of champagne to toast Gemma, Steve and I dashed for our train, collapsing into our seats after a big day on our feet and very little sleep the night before. It wasn't a sad goodbye as I'd have time with Barb in London soon.

Did I mention how hot it was? Walking in the door that night was like stepping into a baking, hot oven. It was still 28 °C and we were sweltering. The fan whirred and whined all night.

Early in June I'd had an email from Anne at the B&B.

"*Every year Hampton Court Palace has a flower show. I've got tickets. You must come, Annemarie. It really is something to see. It's on July 8th. We'll make a day of it, starting with coffee in one of the pavilions. I'm sure we'll end it with a glass of Pimm's! What do you think?*"

What did I think? Of course I'd go. It sounded a gorgeous day out to me.

"*Love to Anne, thank you. I've heard the show is fantastic. I'll pay of course.*"

"*Excellent. I know we could walk but Richard will drop us off as we'll be on our feet all day. We can sort out timing nearer the day. Don't worry about the money right now.*"

Supposedly the Hampton Court Palace Flower Show (organised by the Royal Horticultural Society), is less prestigious than say, the internationally renowned Chelsea Flower Show, but it has become the biggest flower show in the world, in terms of numbers attending and event space. With such a wide variety of exhibits and workshops for the average home gardener, it appealed to a vast audience. What made this show even more appealing was that it was easily accessible by train, with Hampton Court station a five-minute walk from the main gate. It's held over several days and can attract up to 300,000 people.

What a fabulous day. Richard dropped us off while it was still cool, and well before opening time. Anne and I were prepared, wearing loose cotton dresses and armed with wide-brimmed hats, sun lotion and bottles of water. It was going to be another scorcher. London's heatwave was unrelenting.

As soon as the gates opened, Anne and I made a beeline for the coffee cabin with me oohing and aahing at everything on our way. Every stall had a pink banner across the top of it, advertising which nursery or place things were from, and numbered to correspond with our guidebooks. Coffee in hand, we found a seat in the shade and just looked and looked, taking in all the different stalls and cabins, some linked by colourful, flapping bunting, with exquisite colours catching my eye every way I turned. I couldn't wait to get inside the floral marquees, pavilions and show gardens.

"We better move." Anne stood, taking my empty coffee cup. "We've got a big day ahead and it's getting very busy. Look how many have arrived since we sat down." She gestured towards the coffee queue. "Let's get roaming."

I quickly gathered up my stuff and we were off. I fell in love with the overflowing and lively vegetable plots, with every plump, green, red, yellow, edible thing imaginable. One stall was full of citrus fruit and I'm sure the owner had polished the glossy lemons and mandarins – as well as the leaves. Ooh, I just wanted to reach out and .... "No!" Anne, giggling, almost had to slap my hand away, pointing to the sign saying, 'Please do not touch the fruit'. I'm not surprised they needed to tell people. It was so tempting.

Imagine the overwhelming scent, evident when standing at

the entrance to the lily tent. Oh, it was an intense visual and sensory overload. Every colour was available; pure whites, muted pinks, lemon yellow, blues, greens, purples, vibrant orange and the variegated ones too. I overhead a woman telling her friend it was like being 'trapped in a jewellery box'. It was exactly that.

Then there were the orchids, the dahlias, the begonias, the hydrangeas, the foxgloves, the allium, the lavenders – to name a few! Everywhere was a riot of colour and fragrance, with some blooms as large as dinner plates, giving cause to wonder what the grower fed them. Then there were the peonies. One large, dreamy, creamy bunch had been named 'A Bowl of Cream'. They were stunning. It was all so overwhelming but so awe-inspiring at the same time.

Then it was time to explore the set gardens, waterfalls and sculptures. Talent was in abundance and overflowing, with some sculptures so enormous they'd need a large estate to accommodate them. Huge, cut-out steel and patinated orbs were partly opened so visitors could step into an airy seating area made from hewn rock. Giant metal reeds, with glossy, polished stainless-steel leaves, 'grew' out of a lush, green-leafed landscape, creating a great contrast. One of the sculptures was a life-sized galvanised watering can, covered in multi-coloured and joined-up crochet squares. It was very attention-grabbing. Some people were just so creative and clever with their hands.

We found a lovely lunch marquee, tucked ourselves into a shaded and cool corner and nibbled our way through ladylike ham, egg and cress club sandwiches, sharing a chocolate brownie with our second coffee. Anne had her head buried in the catalogue while I sat, cup in hand, observing everyone around us. It was very busy and bustling with the clatter of crockery, cutlery and queues as well as the chatter. People were fanning themselves with the catalogues and mopping brows, it was that warm, and I caught snippets of conversation of who'd seen what, which one they'd loved most so far.

"Okay, I think we'll head down to the ..." I cut Anne off mid-sentence.

"Oh my God, Anne." I grabbed her by the wrist, pointing outside where I'd just seen an elderly man collapse.

People rushed from tables to help. One woman soaked a table napkin with her glass of water and held it to his forehead. Another was on the phone, calling an ambulance, I guessed. Officials raced over with a St John's officer close behind. It had to be the heat. I was hoping it wasn't a heart attack or stroke. It was awful to witness but a few minutes later, he was sitting up.

"He looks okay now and has the right people helping," Anne said, patting my hand. "He'll be fine. Let's head down to see the garden studios. I've always fancied one of those."

"You're right. He's being well looked after," I replied, looking at the medics leaning over the man.

We wandered down one of the many lanes created by the exhibiting stalls lining either side. "A friend of mine, Bridget, is getting one of those studios. She's going to set up her sewing machine and art easel in it. It'll be her 'she-shed' as opposed to a man cave," I told Anne, laughing.

A moment later I added, "This one's mine. Look, Anne. It's gorgeous." This studio was nothing like a she-shed. It was an elegant drawing room with a large scroll-top mirror on the back wall, reflecting the green of the perfectly positioned potted palms and the ornate silver and glass chandelier, hanging from the centre. A long cream-coloured hall table, placed under the mirror, held tall lamps placed on each end, with floral shades in vivid blues, greens and pinks while large, *faux* moss hares perched in between.

Two ornate Queen Anne chairs, upholstered in the same floral fabric as the shades, sat either side of the room. A bookcase filled with glossy-covered gardening books and magazines lined a side wall, and two framed Kew Garden prints completed the elegance of this beautiful studio.

The exterior and multi-paned French doors and windows, painted in the softest sage green, along with the wooden shingle roof, created the perfect finish. Oh, I most certainly had studio envy.

Some of the studios were two-roomed and a lot more modern. Others were set up as rustic garden sheds and filled with neatly stacked and shelved terracotta pots and bases of all sizes. A battered wooden desk, covered in old gardening notebooks, seed packets, plant stakes and what looked like old, cracked railway tea mugs, really looked authentic. The detail even came down to a gentleman's pipe, sitting in an ashtray with a pouch of Old Royal tobacco beside it. It was fabulous and just like the shed I saw in the Palace gardens on an earlier visit. Wait a minute! Maybe they'd just moved it in for the show?

After a few more stalls of classic English pottery and ceramics, I turned to my friend, fanning myself with my catalogue. "It's so hot and I'd like to sit for a while. Time for a refreshing Pimm's, I think, Mrs Steer (Anne)."

"Don't ask me twice!" was all the answer I needed. I took her by the arm and 'steered' her in the direction of the pretty Pimm's tent in the distance.

What a day. Bloomin' marvellous!

The British Museum is another of London's ancient and incredible institutions. It was founded in 1753 and there's always something fascinating to read and interesting to see. And it's free. It's located in the historically fashionable area of Bloomsbury and, according to Wikipedia, 'Its permanent collection of eight million works is amongst the largest and most comprehensive in existence. It documents the story of human culture from its beginnings to the present.'

This visit was to a ticketed event – the Rodin and the Art of Ancient Greece exhibition. We'd been meaning to go for weeks. Mindful of the heat we decided to get there for the opening at 10.00 a.m. but, on our arrival, found there was already a queue of a hundred people or more, all with the same idea. Since our visit to Rodin's Museum and Garden in Paris, way back in 2008, I'd absorbed everything I came across about him and his sculptures. At this exhibition I learned even more.

Rodin's best-known works are probably *The Kiss* and *The Thinker*. These two pieces were originally small figures created to sit on monumental gates (*The Gates of Hell*), commissioned for the entrance to a new decorative arts museum in Paris. Sadly, the museum was never built but Rodin finished the gates, nonetheless. I found Rodin's Garden in Paris to be a spiritual place as his sculptures are so real, expressing great emotion. It's one of those peaceful and restful gardens where you can sit on a bench seat and just take it all in.

It only took us an hour to see the museum exhibition and, after being in a cool and air-conditioned room, the rest of the museum felt overwhelmingly hot. Steve and I whizzed through the Egyptian rooms then got ourselves back out on the street. Sitting having coffee in the shade across the street, we watched hordes of people streaming through the gates to queue in that awful heat, at the beginning of their tour of the museum.

"I'm here!" came the cheery voice down the phone. It was Barb. She'd arrived in London and was staying in town. "I'm getting the train out to Kingston-Upon-Thames in the morning. Okay to meet me there?"

"Perfect, Barb. I can tour you around the gorgeous

boutiques before we get the bus back to Teddington. I've booked a cute restaurant in the High Street for lunch, but I'll run through the day's itinerary while we have coffee in Kingston. See you in the morning!"

I was excited that she was coming out to our neck of the woods. So many lovely spots to show her.

Our day together was full on. We walked and talked our socks off, jumping from one topic to the other, never finishing our sentences as there was so much to catch up on. Lunch at the chic One One Four restaurant in Teddington High Street was divine. We chose the two-course lunch menu and were both impressed with the food – risotto and duck; strawberry bavarois and a cheese plate to share. It was plenty for the two of us. A glass of rosé was our choice; not the correct wine match of course, but we enjoyed it.

On we went to the delightful Petersham Nurseries, snaking our way across the compacted dirt floor through the luxurious soaps and scents, French antiques and furniture, interiors and gardening books and pottery and out to the delights of the garden shop at the rear, which offers beautiful cards and garden journals, artisan garden tools as well as a variety of plants. The 'room' is perfectly described as an oasis of flora.

Leaving Petersham behind, we trekked up Richmond Hill to the lookout point. Barb was so impressed with the view – she couldn't not be. "I can see why you love living here." Barb was shading her eyes with her hand, taking it all in. "There's so much to see and do as well as having all this nature on your doorstep."

"Exactly. We love it. It's hard to decide what to do next," I replied, so happy she could see and understand.

Down the slope we walked and into Richmond itself, through some of the little historic back streets and into the main retail area.

"Ooh, let's pop in here." Something had caught Barb's eye in

Bimba Y Lola, one of the many gorgeous boutiques in the street. Fifteen minutes later we left, a carrier bag slung over Barb's wrist containing a new pair of loafers and a pretty, summery top.

"I do love a sale," she grinned at me. I snorted, knowing just how true that was. I looped my arm through hers, walking her to the bus to head home for a light dinner, before putting her on the train back to London. It had been a super day with my lovely friend and there was more to come.

Two days later I was on the train myself, heading into Waterloo. My Wednesday morning job was postponed as Barb had rung the night before, offering me a ticket to Kensington Palace and the Princess Diana exhibition. I was thrilled to bits. As a young woman I was in awe of Diana, her life, and her clothes, devouring anything and everything ever written about her and, of course, I pored over the photographs.

"Afterwards, I thought we could have a wander down Kensington High Street and treat ourselves to a little lunch," Barbara said. I was up for that. Nothing like a mooch down that gorgeous street and I do love a little ladies' mid-week lunch ...

The exhibition was outstanding. The detail on the dresses and the reasons why Diana chose some fabrics, and some designs, was interesting. As an example, when she visited Saudi Arabia, her dress was embellished with falcons, their native bird, and had a high neckline and long sleeves to respect their customs.

Jasper Conran said of her: "Whenever the Princess discussed her clothes with me, part of it was always, 'What message will I be giving out if I wear this?' For her, that became the real language of clothes."

The photos of Diana as a shy 20-year-old girl about to get married – the young, innocent Diana – show a vastly different person from the woman she blossomed into – a confident, sleek and very sexy woman.

The following words displayed at the beginning of the exhibition summed up her life perfectly.

Diana, Princess of Wales was one of the most famous women of the twentieth century. She combined the allure of royalty with the fascination of international celebrity, and the press commented on every detail of her life and style. The Princess crafted her public image carefully and soon learned how to use it to engage and inspire people all over the world.
The outfits in the exhibition track her evolution as a princess, trend-setter, humanitarian and woman, whose ability to connect with people remains powerful today.

All the dresses were exquisite, starting off so demure and finishing sophisticated and elegant. Year by year she became more sophisticated and surer of herself. I loved this statement of Diana's, which I think a lot of us could relate to: 'Sometimes I can be a little outrageous, which is quite nice. Sometimes.'

With 35 °C forecast for the following day it was time to get out of London. Our destination was Glasgow, the birth city of Steve's mother and grandmother and we were on a mission to find the street they lived in, in the historic Gorbals district.

I know I've said it already, but I just love train travel – no queues, no having to be there two hours before departure, no cancellation because of fog, no security to get through. It's just so much more relaxing than air travel and while it may take longer than a flight, when there's time, that's not a problem and there's an ever-changing landscape.

I was so looking forward to going to Glasgow and staying with Margo and Tom. Margo came to live in New Zealand when she and I were both 19. She worked with my sister in Wellington and, because of difficult circumstances, came to live with us for four months.

Back then in New Zealand there were no international free trade agreements, the aim being to create industry and jobs internally. Therefore, some imported goods incurred a hefty tariff. Clothing was one of those industries. Margo arrived at ours with the most amazing wardrobe, stashed into two huge suitcases. We were the same size and she let my sister and me wear whatever we wanted to borrow. For a young girl this was terribly exciting, and it was very much 'first up, best dressed' in our house. Margo and I have stayed in touch over the years, and I went and stayed with her and Tom at the age of 23, then she and Tom came to visit us in Auckland 30 years later. When she discovered we were going to live in London, she quickly invited us to go and stay with them in Glasgow when we got the chance.

Whoever said Glasgow has terrible weather presumably made that up. Our first day out on the Hop On, Hop Off bus was a stunner – vivid blue sky, bright sunshine and warm. Yes, warm! Standing in the bus queue waiting to pay, we got to experience first-hand the kindness of strangers. Two women got off the bus at the end of their tour and approached us.

"Would you like these?" one of the women asked, holding out two tickets for the tour bus. "We won't be going around again and there's the rest of the day left."

"Oh, how fabulous. And very generous of you. Thank you very much." I smiled at them both, gladly accepting the tickets. I'd 'pay it forward' when I got the opportunity.

"A pleasure. No point in wasting them. Enjoy the tour," she said. And with a wave of their hands the two of them tottered off down the street.

"Well that was very kind," I said to Steve, once we were seated.

"Yep. Certainly was." Steve was already absorbed in the spectacular architecture and murals, old and modern dotted all over the city.

Most of Glasgow's architecture can be attributed to Charles Rennie MacIntosh, born into a working-class family on 7 June 1868. Charles honed his creative talents at night classes at the Glasgow School of Art and while apprenticed to Honeyman and Keppie – one of Glasgow's major architectural firms. A colleague, Herbert McNair, and Charles met two sisters; Frances and Margaret Macdonald. Herbert married Frances, and Charles, Margaret. They became known as 'The Four' and, while at the Glasgow School of Art, established what is called 'The Glasgow Style' – an art movement that ran from the 1890s to approximately 1914, utilising a stunning Art Nouveau style and introducing over seventy other designers to it.

Charles' style was modern and innovative for the time, definitely not reflecting the era he lived in. He was certainly no ordinary young man and his style made him stand out amongst his peers. As is often the case with artists of all genres, his work wasn't totally appreciated until after his death. He struggled through financial losses, addiction to alcohol, and suffered from depression. After several moves he and Margaret settled in London, and Charles spent his later years painting watercolours. He passed away in 1928.

At the end of our bus tour, we headed for the Kelvingrove Art Gallery and Museum. It holds many fabulous artworks including Renaissance paintings and Egyptian artefacts and was highly recommended. The building itself is very beautiful and worth a visit for that alone, but the interior architecture and exhibits require hours to see and absorb. Sadly, we couldn't do it all justice but did get to spend a couple of hours trawling through the many galleries.

Late in the afternoon I tapped an engrossed Steve on the elbow. "Time to go. We've got to get back to the station and catch the five o'clock train. Tom's coming home early today, specially."

"Oh, right. I'll just finish reading this. I'll meet you at the front entrance in a few minutes."

I could hear music on my way to the foyer and, passing the main auditorium, I caught a few minutes of the pipe organ recital while I waited for Steve to catch up. Reading the brochure blurb on the train I learned that the magnificent pipe organ was installed over a hundred years ago. It was very impressive.

Upstairs, after a lovely evening catching up with Tom and Margo, Steve and I were getting ready for bed. "We're out for the day with Tom and Margo on Saturday, so let's go tomorrow to see if we can find exactly where mum was born and she and Nanny lived," Steve suggested. "I've looked up how to get there but we can check it with Margo in the morning."

I pulled the covers back and climbed into bed. "OK, sounds good," I yawned. We'd stayed up late chatting and I was ready for sleep. "Do I need to set the alarm? I'm about to switch off the light."

"No, we'll hear Tom get up for work, so we'll stir then. Night, night."

The reason Steve and I were able to move to London so easily was all thanks to his mother being born in Scotland (i.e., the UK), meaning that Steve was able to get a British passport. Thank you, Maureen.

Maureen was born in 1938 into a poverty-stricken tenement slum on the south bank of the River Clyde, in an area known as The Gorbals. Living conditions were appalling and families of up to eight crammed into one room, known as a 'single end'. It was common for thirty people to share a toilet, and forty to share one tap. At one time, sewage ran through the streets. No one I know could even begin to imagine how to live like that, with the expectation nowadays of having two toilets, at least.

The children though, were oblivious and just got on with life, playing in the streets in muddy puddles and using a tin as a football, setting up games wherever they could.

There were no laundry facilities in the tenements. The women would load up the washing in their old prams and wheel it down the street to the wash house, known as 'the steamie'. Here, women bonded over the hot, wet clothes as they scrubbed, sharing any family news, gossip and scandal. Men bonded at the pub and had the football to yarn about.

Despite the awful living conditions, people from The Gorbals were known for their community spirit and togetherness during the toughest of times. Mind you, it was best to steer well clear of the area late at night.

"Well, this is the right street," Steve said looking at the map, rather puzzled as to why we couldn't find No. 24.

"You can see how modern it is now, though. Maybe the rest of the street got demolished," I suggested, making my way to the end of it, to see if there was a different name on that signpost.

Two wee Glasgow women were coming towards us, blethering away together, their arms linked, with a handbag slung over their free one.

"Are ye awright, hen?" one of them asked, as we arrived side by side. "Ye're lookin' a wee bit lost. Can we help ye?"

"Thank you, yes. You see, my husband," I turned indicating Steve, "and I are from New Zealand and we're trying to find No. 24. Steve's mother was born here, in this street, but we've been up and down a few times and can't find it. The street just seems to peter out."

"Och, pet that's awfy sad," she said, patting Steve on the arm. "Ye've come an awfy lang way."

I wasn't about to launch into an explanation of having come up from London on the train, not just flown in from New Zealand.

"Ye'll noo doubt know that this was The Gorbals, and the ol' tenements got demolished, ooh let's see, way back in the 1950s. Let me think," she paused, a frown wrinkling her brow. "Connie, do ye think No. 24 could 'a been where the whisky distillery is noo?" she asked her friend, waving her free arm and handbag in the direction of giant vats covering a vast area across the street.

"Och, aye. I'd say so." Connie squinted across the street at the vats. "I cannae remember when they were built, but it's an awfie lang time ago noo, in't it, Ellie," she said, nodding at the woman who first spoke to us.

"Och, aye, och aye." Ellie pondered a minute. "I'll tell ye what. If you'd like tae ken more aboot the area, take yerselves into the People's Palace. It's a braw place. Aye, it is that. Ye'll find all ye need to know aboot life in The Gorbals. It's ower there in Glesca Green," she said, waving in no particular direction. "It's got a gorgeous wee winter garden too. Ye must go and hae a wee look while ye're here."

It was so lovely hearing that Glaswegian accent. Steve and I couldn't help but grin at each other, remembering Allan and Nessie (and Barb's) Scottishness. These two were true 'Weegies' – a term used to describe Glaswegians. I couldn't understand half of what they said but got the gist of it.

"Now, pet," Ellie said to me, "have ye had a wee cake and coffee this mornin? If no, pop along to the wee Italian café. Och, he makes the best coffee, and the cakes are a wee bit o' heaven. Enjoy."

"Well, you two were a joy to meet!" I bent and gave them each a quick hug. "Thank you so much for being so nice and friendly."

"Yes, thanks for your help." Steve smiled at them and gently shook their hands. "We'll have a coffee first and maybe that 'wee' cake too before we explore the People's Palace."

Off they went, arms re-linked, turning to give us a wave and resuming their non-stop 'blethering'. So sweet.

With great Illy coffee drunk and two cannoli pastries demolished, we got directions to the People's Palace from the lovely Italian man behind the café counter.

What a stunning building. An adaptation of the French Renaissance style, the People's Palace sits perfectly on the Glasgow Green with a beautiful ornate terracotta fountain on one side and a magnificent steel and glass greenhouse on the other. The fountain is supposedly the largest terracotta fountain in the world made by the ceramics company Royal Doulton for the Glasgow Exhibition of 1888.

The general theme of the fountain glorifies the British Empire. Queen Victoria stands atop the centre of the fountain, symbolising her reign over the empire. Directly below her are water-carrying maids, emptying water onto the lower tiers. One level down is a sailor and one soldier from each of Scotland, England and Wales, the source of Victoria's glory. On the lowest tier sit four groups of figures, representing the four major colonies of the empire, South Africa, Australia, Canada and India. Little ol' New Zealand is not a 'major' colony and doesn't get a look-in.

Both the exterior and interior architecture of the Palace were fabulous, and the museum collection tells the social history of the people and the city from about 1750 onwards. It was fascinating. The People's Palace Museum and Glasshouse was built for the people of the East End of Glasgow as a cultural centre and garden so that those living in unhealthy and overcrowded conditions would have a place of beauty to visit.

"Did you know much about where Maureen and Nanny lived, before we went to the People's Palace?" I looked up at Steve, taking his arm on our walk back to the bus.

"Mum didn't really talk about it. I think she wanted to put it behind her and get on with her New Zealand life."

From the little we do know, Maureen and her younger brother Jimmy were casualties of what is known as Britain's Child Migrant Programme and were put on a ship in 1947 at the ages of 9 and 7 respectively, sailing for six weeks from London to Wellington, New Zealand. Yes, it's hard to believe, isn't it?

Nanny (Jenny), Steve's grandmother, and her four young children had been abandoned in The Gorbals by his grandfather. He'd decided it was too hard being a father and just left. Jenny got work in a nearby factory for several years but was still on the breadline and just couldn't make ends meet, with four mouths to feed as well as herself. Then, to rain further blows on the poor woman, Jenny was 'let go' from the factory. On her way home that evening, feeling sick to her stomach with worry about how she was going to feed the children, she saw a poster plastered to a lamppost: Send Your Children To A Better Life In New Zealand.

Checking her purse, Jenny had something like two shillings to her name. The tears must have been running down her face in despair about her financial state. The two older children were old enough to earn a few 'bob' and to help. Jenny made the hardest decision of her life – to send her youngest two to New Zealand for what she believed would be a better life.

When I first heard this story, I was filled with horror. How could anyone do that to their children? It was so abhorrent to me. But put yourself in Jenny's place. She truly believed they would be better off out of the slums, poverty and subsequent poor health and deprivation. New Zealand was painted in glowing colours, the land of milk and honey and fresh air. Well, it most likely was then – but remember, there are nasty people all over the world and New Zealand was no different.

After what would have been heart-wrenching goodbyes, the children left Scotland, never knowing when they would see their mother and brothers again. It gets worse. When the children finally arrived in Wellington the authorities separated them. Maureen went with one family and Jimmy with another – yet more seemingly unendurable agony for the children.

What I think to be true is that Maureen went to a farming family where she had to be up at the crack of dawn to get her chores done before she walked to school. After school, it was the same scenario until she went to bed. Steve doesn't think she was physically abused but there didn't seem to have been a lot of care or love. Some of these families only took the children in so that there would be an extra pair of hands to do the work.

At the age of 18, Maureen married Steve's dad, Rex, and the following year Steve was born. Steve doesn't remember when Jenny came out to New Zealand with the two older children but does remember special times of going to stay with his Nanny when he was little, in Titahi Bay, near Wellington. We tried to work out how long it would have been before Maureen met her mother again and calculated it was about 15 years. Was it a stilted reunion – two women who didn't really know each other? Or was it a loving embrace, full of tears for the unknown years of each other's lives? We just don't know as Steve is the only surviving family member. Whatever the circumstances, it was incredibly sad.

Maureen and Jimmy were just two of thousands of children who were sent away. They were escaping poverty and Jenny thought they would be well cared for and well fed. Other children came from institutions and orphanages and were put into something similar in Australia. Some were told that their parents were dead. I've done a little research and I quote: 'Between 1922 and 1967 about 150,000 children, with an average age of eight years and nine months, were shipped from Great Britain to help populate the British Dominions of Canada, Rhodesia, New Zealand and Australia with "good white stock."' I do know that recently there has been an apology from the Australian Government for what was done, and the UK has paid compensation. Too little, too late for Maureen and Jimmy and shocking, to say the least.

"Would ye hurry up youse two and ge' yerselves doon the stairs!" Tom hollered up at us. "We're leaving the hoose in five." Tom has a very thick Glaswegian accent and at times I've had to turn to Margo and ask, "What did he say, what did he say?" But I understood that instruction very clearly!

"Coming!" I yelled back, grabbing my bag, and scrambling down the stairs to find Tom and Margo waiting patiently at the back door. Steve was still faffing about, getting his shoes on in the bedroom.

Tom was driving us to Falkirk to see the famous Kelpies and the Falkirk Wheel. The Kelpies are a monument to horse-powered heritage across Central Scotland. These incredible steel structures stand a colossal 90 feet above the Forth and Clyde Canal, in beautiful parkland known as the Helix. Each one weighs nearly 300 tons. They are a magnificent sight and people standing beside them look Lilliputian in comparison. Only those booked on a Kelpies tour can step inside to witness the complexity of their engineering. These are the largest equine sculptures in the world.

Getting back to the car was tricky. "Watch yerself, Annemarie." Tom nodded at the swan waddling up the path ahead of us, corralling her cygnets. "She's nippin at anything and everything. Tha' wee dog just got pecked, poor wee bugger."

The young couple in front were now carrying their shivering little poodle, trying to console it after its ordeal. They slid down the bank to avoid getting a nip themselves and we followed shortly after them. 'Mum' was very fierce, protecting her babies while she tried to get them down into the water.

Margo, in the front seat, looked at her watch. "Tom, I think we need a coffee and a scone before we look at the Falkirk Wheel. We're too early for the next lift," she announced.

"Nae a problem, me darlin'. Let's do that." Tom grinned at her, patting her on the leg. He was always so genial. "Youse two keen?" he asked us in the rear-view mirror.

"Always. Definitely." We both nodded at him.

The announcement came over the intercom that the next lift would be in five minutes. Perfect timing as we'd demolished our coffees and scones and were ready. After a quick loo stop we were out on the patio with an expectant group, all eyes on this incredible feat of engineering, waiting for it to move.

The Falkirk Wheel is a gargantuan boatlift, connecting the Forth and Clyde and Union Canals, lifting or dropping the boats some 115 feet and taking only five minutes to do so. Before the wheel was installed the boats had to enter and exit eleven locks, which took most of a day and would have been so tedious. The cost of building the wheel was a whopping £17 million – and that was only a third of the cost for the whole restoration. It was very impressive to watch in action.

Back at the car, Tom clicked the remote to open the doors. He stopped and looked at us. "Hae you two ever set foot on St Andrews golf course in Fife?"

"Ah, no, we've never been. It's a special place, according to our friends, Barb and Gerard and golfers around the world," answered Steve.

"Margo, is there anything we hae to do the noon?"

"No, Tom, no, nothing. Maybe a walk, but that's it."

"Okay then." Tom slid into the driver's seat. "We're away to St Andrews. Strap yerselves in. It's only an hour and a half away!"

Decision made, Tom swung the car around and assiduously drove the line to St Andrews, taking us through villages and towns that I'd only ever heard about from Barb, with a hoick in her throat as she pronounced them – Pitlochry, Auchterarder, Auchtermuchty. I can already hear you trying to pronounce them!

Steve was very excited. Since around the year 1400, golf has been played on the hallowed ground of St Andrews links. Six 18-hole golf courses have now been carved out of the landscape and golfing pilgrims from around the world revere this place as being almost 'biblical' in golfing circles. It's not all golf though, as St Andrews is also the home of an old and world-class university.

After a lovely ramble through the main street and a sandwich lunch, Tom walked us to the outskirts of the town. "I want to show youse something." He crooked his finger at us, indicating we should follow.

A few minutes later we stood gaping, taking in the incredible view and crumbling, ancient stone ruins of a medieval cathedral and cemetery, situated on the cliff top and overlooking the bay and the North Sea. One tower, a side wall and an end gable still stood, and the grounds were carved out to show the original layout of the church, which had its origins in 1158. It fell into ruin during the Scottish Reformation around 1560. Over the centuries, stones have been removed from the site for use in other buildings in the town, but a stop was put to this in the mid-nineteenth century. It's a magnificent, almost eerie sight and, with my vivid imagination, I could almost sense life at that time, happening around me.

Tom is a walking encyclopaedia. He was able to give us dates, names and stories about the historic site we were standing on. His knowledge of so many things in history is incredible and nothing is ever told to impress; he just wants to share with others an understanding of what they see, which was brilliant for us.

The path around the clifftops gave magical and seemingly endless, sweeping views out to sea and of the beautiful grey stone buildings of the town on the other side of the road; some with climbing ivy clinging to the sides. High, mossy stone walls with turreted column entranceways surrounded some of the historic grey stone university buildings, adding to the elegant ambiance of the town. Everywhere we turned there was something architectural punctuating the timeless streets of the town.

"There you go!" said Tom, throwing his arms wide to take in the glorious green golf course of St Andrews. "And look at the clubhouse. So beautiful." I could hear the admiration in his voice.

It was beautiful – all of it. The course looked immaculately groomed and the clubhouse so imposing.

"This clubhouse has been here since 1854 and is known architecturally as the neo-classical style. The first tee is right in front of it, near the flag you can see on the adjacent green." Tom pointed to a flag, flapping in the afternoon sea breeze. "Your pals could sit sipping a pint or a wee gin and tonic and watch you begin your 18 holes. The most famous 18 holes in the world."

Steve was itching to get closer. "Let's see if we can go in the gate for a bit of a wander round. Looks like a tournament is on. C'mon."

No one was bothered as we walked in. Tickets were needed for the seated area, but we were just having a look and that was enough to keep Steve happy. How he would have loved to trundle his clubs around that course. Maybe one day.

It was a soggy day when our train from Glasgow pulled into Edinburgh's Waverley station. Spilling out onto the platform and into the street were hundreds of tourists, just like us, attempting to stay dry. It was a push-and-shove affair up the

Royal Mile and into the Castle grounds, trying to avoid having an eye gouged out by the many umbrellas being thrust up.

The tiered seating was already up in the castle forecourt in preparation for the famous Tattoo, two days away. Sadly, it created an ugly and obliterating view of the castle entrance. The weather didn't help and, when the man in front of me in the ticket office collected tickets for the jostling and noisy gaggle of school children waiting outside, I left the queue and joined Steve, who was waiting under an umbrella.

"It's all too hectic in there," I grumbled. "And this lot," I nodded at the kids pushing and shoving, "are in next. I think I'll just look at online pictures."

Steve wasn't bothered about not going in. "We've done a few castles in our time. Let's get back down the Mile and find a café off the beaten track and have a coffee. Hopefully the rain will have eased by then and we can just walk the streets for a while."

After a damp journey around the city on the Sunday Hop On/Hop Off bus, admiring this city's architecture, we spent the afternoon ducking in and out of busy galleries and museums. Lots of other tourists had the same idea and were just sitting where they could, out of the rain, not even bothering to look around. It was a 'dreich' day, as they say in Scotland. I had tried to 'pay it forward' and give our Edinburgh bus tickets away as they had a half day left on them, but people were very suspicious of me, giving me filthy looks and brushing me off. After four rejections, I gave up and dumped them in a bin.

A warm sun finally shone on us, waiting in line for Holyrood Palace to open. Also known as Holyroodhouse, this is the official Scottish residence of the British monarch. The Mary Queen of Scots sixteenth-century apartments and the state apartments were open for public viewing. That's what we'd come to see, and we were warmly welcomed by guides wearing an ancient Stewart hunting tartan, in both trousers and kilts –

rich greens and blues with vertical and horizontal yellow stripes. Matched with navy cloaks with the same tartan collar, the guides looked very smart and elegant.

Ornate black and gold lamps hung high on either side of one entrance were captivating. Out on the street, I'd caught a glimpse of a lamppost with an octagonal wrought-iron and glass shade with a very cute little metal, gold and red crown on the top. These gave a sense of history and royalty to the area.

Using the audio-guide it was a great tour throughout but, heavens, there were some dreadful deeds committed there. Back in the day it was very easy to be labelled a traitor, found guilty of treason (no proof needed) and be locked up for life, or executed. People needed to be extremely careful about what they said or did.

Queen Elizabeth II went to Holyrood for a week every year during the summer for official engagements and entertaining. She'd been there the first week in July and I bet she was really upset at missing us by a couple of weeks!

"Had enough gore and horrors for one morning?" Steve asked me, dropping his headset into the box at the exit.

"Poor Rizzio! What a dreadful end he had. And what about Mary's husband? What was his name? A right bastard and nasty piece of work." I shuddered, remembering the story of the horrific murder of David Rizzio, Mary Queen of Scots' secretary and advisor.

"He was called Darnley. Lord Darnley – otherwise Henry Stuart, her cousin no less," Steve informed me, leading me out the door and into the courtyard.

"Do you think you could cope with a cheese scone and coffee? The café's across the way there." He pointed over to the Mews Courtyard. "It's warm enough to sit outside."

"Oooh that looks so pretty." The tall, square-cut box hedges were planted into elegant, white timber boxes and the multi-paned white French doors and windows of the café were opened to the sunshine. Large, square cream-coloured umbrellas gave shade to the outdoor table settings. Everything looked fresh and inviting.

"Hurry up, then." I grabbed Steve by the arm, hauling him across the driveway. As soon as I'd finished my coffee and scone, I said to Steve, "I'm just popping into the shop for a minute, before we leave. I'll be out shortly." I quickly scampered off to the Queen's Gallery gift shop, trying to shake him off so I could have a lovely look around. Most people can never, ever leave a castle, palace, museum or art gallery without exiting through the gift shop – well I can't. I love them.

"Hang on. I'll come too." Steve called, getting to his feet. Oh no. I thought I'd get a quiet mooch and a possible purchase without the 'handbrake'. No such luck.

The gift shop was an absolute treasure trove of teas, biscuits, homeware, books, jewellery – I could have bought a tiara and been crowned the Queen of Nothing ... What grabbed me most was the china. Cups and saucers, mugs, teapots, milk jugs, sugar bowls – all gorgeous with an engraved coats of arms, or monogrammed and painted in golds, pinks, blues and greens in filigree patterns.

I stopped in front of a tea set. Four gorgeous large cups and saucers, each one in a different shade of pastel pink, blue, yellow and green, with a gold latticework pattern over the top, were nestled in a froth of white satin and encased in a wooden, gold-coloured presentation box. They were divine. I turned the tag over to see the price. £500 – that's NZ$1,000! I nearly died. The sharp intake of breath from over my shoulder warned me that Steve was standing behind me.

"Oh, I'd just love this," I said wistfully, turning to look at him. The colour had almost drained from Steve's face and he looked at me as if I'd lost my mind and a van would arrive at any moment to whisk me off to a home for the bewildered. I'm sure you could picture it all.

"Don't worry," I reassured him, patting him on the arm. "I'm not going to buy it." His relief was palpable, realising I'd come to my senses, and his colour returned.

When I posted the cups and saucers on Facebook, telling the girls how much I wanted them but had 'the handbrake' with me, my sister Jill quipped, "Well, take the handbrake off!" I laughed and laughed. Another, ever-practical friend replied, "Don't bother. You can't put them in the dishwasher." The dream was lovely while it lasted.

Holyroodhouse really is rather breathtaking to see, as are the gardens and ruins of Holyrood Abbey, which stand next to the Palace, overlooked by the spectacular Salisbury Crags. Just a short walk from there is Holyrood Park, a wild and wondrous area, full of unique flora and fauna. The park is home to ancient volcanoes and phenomenal geological sites. Looking up, people hiking up the path cut into the crags to see the preserved fort on Arthur's Seat, seemed like marching ants, they were that insignificant against the rugged backdrop. The panoramic views from the top are supposed to be fantastic. There just wasn't the time, and we were wrongly dressed, to climb the path ourselves, as much as we'd both have liked to.

We jumped several centuries by crossing the road from the Palace to the Scottish Parliament. This extremely modern building has only been there since 2004 and, even though it was architecturally designed and built, I felt it was totally out of place and unsympathetic to its surroundings. Just my humble opinion, of course. Inside it felt like a rabbit warren with many corridors and staircases, but I did think the debating chamber a great space.

Walking back to the main bus station, through the myriad of little alleyways and major streets, our necks were getting sore, looking up at and admiring this and that. Down one little street, we came across an imposing, ancient iron-studded door. A stone plaque above it had an image of a rooster and bore the date 1633. A sign indicated that it was an old brothel and that a ledger/register was kept, recording the names of the prostitutes, a description of what they looked like and other 'attributes' they may have had. Extraordinary, but funny.

One particularly striking building was the enormous Balmoral Hotel with its tall, imposing Gothic clock tower. It's said that the clock hasn't kept proper time since 1902, when the hotel was originally known as the North British Station Hotel. The hotel, like most of the buildings we saw in Glasgow and Edinburgh, had been cleaned of centuries of engrained black soot and smoke, and the original and beautiful stone now shone through.

Our B&B host recommended and booked us into a tiny restaurant for dinner, in Pilrig Street. What a little gem. It was called The Walnut and I could have eaten any of the choices offered on the compact menu. Best of all, it was a BYO and only a couple of doors down from a supermarket where we grabbed a bottle of wine. The food was outstanding. Reservations were definitely needed, as people kept arriving trying to get a table but were turned away. We got lucky.

The July heatwave was relentless. There'd been no rain since the end of May, which was unheard of for London. We practically lived in the park, sitting in the shade and catching the breeze beside the river. That bench seat needed our name engraved on it, we sat there so often.

Lots of others had the same idea, sprawled out on the grass and opening out picnic dinners. We'd be there after dinner too, watching the bird and human life on the Thames at the end of the day. The swans were so entertaining, flying in so gracefully then thrusting their webbed feet straight out, braking hard as they almost crash-landed on the water, wings flapping madly.

They'd then glide like ballerinas to the concrete ramp, waddle up and attend to a bit of last-minute grooming before tucking their heads under their wings for the night. There was always something happening, and the lock keeper was kept busy with so many boats going in and out.

We'd watch the sky turn a golden yellow then blush pink, morphing into red, as the sun dipped down behind the houses. It was time for bed.

I'd opened our windows as wide as possible, trying to cool the flat down and, walking back in one evening, found a green parrot sitting stunned on our windowsill. He looked to have clipped his wing on the edge of the window and there was a drop of blood beside him. Steve managed to cover him quickly with a tea towel and get him back out on the ledge. He flew off perfectly fine. So, the saying 'you can't fly on one wing' just isn't true!

July Snippets

Dorneywood is a delightful eighteenth-century house near Burnham in southern Buckinghamshire. Originally a Georgian farmhouse, it was rebuilt after a fire in 1910 and given to the National Trust by Lord Courtauld-Thomson in 1947 as a country home for a senior member of the government, usually a Secretary of State or Minister of the Crown. When we were there, it was the Chancellor of the Exchequer's country residence and only open to the public on a few days during summer. It wasn't a large house, but obviously very tastefully decorated and comfortable. I could see myself settling into one of the big armchairs beside a roaring fire in the winter, a glass of red wine in hand, after a day's ramble in the countryside.

Anne and Richard had secured tickets for us all to tour the house and gardens, so we decided to make a day of it and booked a lunch at the Blackwood Arms in Burnham – a traditional British country pub serving locally sourced food and great beer – according to Steve and Richard. Anne and I refreshed ourselves with a glass or two of Pimm's. The Blackwood Arms is almost hidden away but was a great find with a fabulous menu.

Late one afternoon, Steve walked in with a bottle of champagne. "Anne and Richard are on their way," he bellowed down the hallway. "We're celebrating!" He held the champagne above his head and let out a whoop.

"Brilliant Steve. You got it! Well done." **Steve had a job** and would start at the beginning of August. No, it wasn't in the fire risk assessment business. He would be the Operations Manager for a small conference company – in Teddington. He had the shortest commute known to man – 10 minutes, on foot. He'd been contacted by a recruitment agency, which had found him via LinkedIn, and after a couple of interviews the job was his. It was only a six-month assignment, but we were ecstatic and, even though the salary wasn't huge, it was enough to cover our monthly living expenses. That's all we needed.

Anne and Richard came through the door, Steve popped the top off the champagne and the bubbles flowed. We raised our glasses with a gleeful 'Cheers!' It was the start of a great job that ended up being extended out to a year.

Delicious tapas at **Morito in Exmouth Market, Clerkenwell** with friends. As we came away The Church of the Holy Redeemer was lit up and looked so inviting in the evening light that I had to go in. A choir was practising, and their voices radiated and lifted to the rafters. Goosebumps came up on my arms.

Friends **Kerry and Jill from Auckland**, touring England, came for dinner, bringing French memories with them in the form of huge, golden sunflowers.

The BP Portrait Awards at the National Gallery and coffee with Mary. I was bewitched by the winning portrait, painted by Miriam Escofet of her mother. Titled *An Angel at my Table* it shows her elderly mother at her kitchen table surrounded by afternoon tea crockery. The light and technique made her mother lifelike. It was beautiful and Escofet said she wanted to 'transmit an idea of the Universal Mother, who is at the centre of our psyche and emotional world'. The BP Portrait Award is the most prestigious portrait painting competition in the world and represents the very best in contemporary portrait painting.

Maryann and Bruce flew in from New York and we had a fab evening of non-stop chat and dinner at Westminster Kitchen in Waterloo.

A quick coffee in Windsor en route to Ascot to do a de-cluttering job with my boss. Stunning blue sky on a hot day. Windsor is so close for us to get to by train. It's now on the list for a day trip with Steve.

Dinner with Murdoch, Kerry L. and friends at The Sands End, Fulham. Another great night.

And the best news I've saved until the end – **my little sister, Jill**

is coming to London with her husband Ferg, for a visit mid-September. I'm so excited! We always have fun.

The following link will take you directly to photos associated with July. Feel free to comment on any of them.

https://bit.ly/LLA_July-2018

AUGUST 2018

TEDDINGTON LIFE; LYVEDEN; ROCKINGHAM CASTLE; A SPECIAL LUNCH AT MANOIR AUX QUAT'SAISONS; CONCOURS D'ELEGANCE

There's no rest for the wicked and I was straight back into work the day after we returned from Edinburgh. I still had plenty of free time to enjoy life and get out and about in the deliciously warm August weather.

We both loved our walks over the Lock Bridge and down the Thames Path to Kingston to get our shopping. Steve always carried Cruella de Vil, our dalmatian-spotted trolley, on his shoulder until we filled her at Aldi then dragged her along the road and bussed home. We'd found several good routes for walking, one taking us in the other direction, through Bushy Park to say good morning to the magnificent deer, then out Shaef (an acronym for Supreme Headquarters of the Allied Expeditionary Forces) Gate, over the railway bridge at the station and back into the High Street and home. This was always a good hour's walk with a welcome coffee stop at the end.

Since we'd arrived, I'd fallen in love with a classy women's boutique, called Nova Fortuny, in the High Street. The dresses in the window were both beautiful and elegant and, with each window change, I'd photograph them and post them on my Facebook page, asking the girls which one they liked; who'd wear what. Everyone joined in with a quip here and there. It was a bit of fun and, if a month had gone by and I hadn't posted any dresses, I'd get a message asking where they were, and had I bought one yet? The price of them was out of my reach so I hadn't purchased a thing, but I did love to stop and look. There was an equivalent men's shop in Kingston (Modigliani) and Steve would drool at the floral shirts in that window. £130 was just a bit steep for a shirt. Still, they were lovely to look at.

August is the month for the annual garden lunch party at Anne and Richard's, and this year we were honoured to be asked to attend. Luckily it was a beautiful Saturday, almost verging on too hot. Steve went round early to help Richard set up tables and umbrellas and put out chairs in the best shady spots on the terrace and in the garden. Thirty of us were going to sit down to a late lunch, and I couldn't turn up empty-handed, knowing what goes into creating a lunch for a lot of people.

Anne had agreed that I could bring a dessert and, knowing how many would be there, I made two huge, sandwiched, hazelnut meringues – one filled with a vanilla cream and the other with lemon curd cream. Lashings of more cream and blueberries, strawberries and kiwi fruit graced the tops. Scattered toasted, slivered almonds finished them off beautifully. What a brilliant time we had with everyone; there was lots of laughing, the music played, the wine flowed. *And the food was amazing.* Other people brought food too, but Anne did most of the mains. She's a fabulous cook. After some mad evening dancing on the lawn, I think it was almost 9.30 p.m. before we got home, falling first into the shower and then into bed. I was very happy with our world.

We had a brunch date with Murdoch the next day, at Beany

Green, a great Australian-inspired café in Sheldon Square, known for its healthy foods and close to Paddington station and Little Venice on Regent's Canal.

I couldn't help but give Paddington Bear a little rub on his nose when we passed him on Platform 1. It was obvious we weren't the first to do so since the bronze statue of him and his suitcase were installed in February 2000. His nose and the brim of his hat were very shiny from so much love.

Sheldon Square is a massive redevelopment that is not only home to high-rise buildings and global companies like Microsoft and Vodafone, but also contains large green spaces, gyms, cafés, restaurants and bars for the many people who work there. It's a thriving community.

"Hi mum, dad. Good to see you." Murdoch arrived and hugged us both. It was always special to meet up with him, and time together was precious. "Let's go eat. I'm starving." God, he sounded just like his father – always hungry.

Murdoch steered us into the doorway of Beany Green, giving his name to the *maitre'd* who guided us to our table. One coffee down and it wasn't long before I had a plate of healthy goodness put in front of me – smashed avocado, a poached egg, chili pesto and two corn fritters. Ribbons of cucumber decorated the plate. Second coffee and much chat later we were back out the door.

"Want to walk down to Little Venice and see the canal boats?" Murdoch asked. "Have you been here before?"

"No," we both piped up. "But I did Google it when we booked the café and was going to suggest we take a walk there," I added. "Good idea. It looks so colourful."

Little Venice was supposedly named by Lord Byron as a joke; others say the poet Robert Browning moved into the area when he returned from Italy and referred to it in that way. Regardless, it was very pretty, walking the canal path and looking at all the brightly painted barges, some of which were like the old gypsy wagons, with terracotta pots spilling colourful flowers and dotting the decks. Some of these were permanent homes. One boat, tied up alongside the path, had been converted into the Waterside Café and fitted out with tables and chairs. The path was very busy and bustling, everyone moving in single file, so as not to bump or knock someone into the canal.

With the intense heat there'd been an explosion of duckweed on the water, turning the canal a vibrant green. The same thing happened in 2016 when dogs were apparently falling into the water, mistaking the green colour for actual lawn. Bizarre.

A few days later we were back on the train, off for another hectic weekend with Bridget and Richard.

Friday night in Gretton became known as Blue Bell night. Shut the front door, totter down the path, cross the road, take ten paces and step inside the Blue Bell Inn. It was *déjà vu*! Once again, the locals welcomed us with open arms. An enormous rhubarb gin and ginger ale arrived in front of me, followed by a zinfandel rosé, both washed down with lots of chat and laughter.

"Shift yourselves, then." Richard thumped his empty beer glass down and was on his feet. "I need to finish off the curries, so it's time to leave." I looked at my watch. Gosh, time flies when you're having fun.

"Yes, boss. We're coming," I saluted Richard, and Bridget and Steve rose with me, all of us draining our wine glasses, and headed for the door.

Richard is famous amongst his friends for his curries and Steve and I awarded him gold that night. They were sensational, worthy of a place on any quality Indian restaurant menu and perfect with a bottle of Grüner Veltliner too.

Once again, we were treated to an elegant Bridget and Richard breakfast table before our trip into the countryside to visit Lyveden. This is not so much a ruin but an unfinished lodge created by Sir Thomas Tresham between 1595 and his death in 1605. The lodge is decorated in detail with religious symbolism, a lot of which is still decipherable today. Thomas was a madly devout Catholic and his religion was part of his every waking moment. His son, Francis, was involved in the famous Gunpowder Plot and died mysteriously of 'unknown causes' in the Tower of London. He was later decapitated, his head placed on a spike at the gates of Northampton. "My God, they were a gruesome lot back then," I said quietly to Steve, shuddering.

Surprisingly, that night I was allowed in the kitchen to create dessert. Last time we'd stayed we'd ended up having a raucous evening with some of Bridget and Richard's friends and they were returning, anticipating an equally fun-filled night. Bridget produced yet another sumptuous main course. It was just expected now!

My huge, individual meringues graced each plate. Before putting them in the oven to bake, I used the back of a dessert spoon to create a scoop to hold the lemon curd cream, topped with strawberries, raspberries and kiwi fruit and a sprinkling of chopped roasted almonds that I would add, once cooked and cooled. They came out well and what I thought was too big for one person got devoured by each and every one of them. Success.

I'm embarrassed to say the evening degenerated (just like last time) as the gang tried to teach Steve and me how to play the card game, Shithead. It was hilarious and so much fun. Too much wine had been drunk to concentrate properly and a good deal of jibes and hectoring ensued.

Our adventure the next day was out to Rockingham Castle, only 10 minutes from Bridget and Richard's. Some parts of this castle date back to 1070. It has now been in the Watson family for 450 years. The views from the top of the tower spill out over farmlands, forests and lush green fields, extending to the horizon.

An extremely knowledgeable guide took us through the beautiful garden and not only told us all about it, but about the ten kings who had sat down to dinner in the Great Hall. The most outstanding part of the garden was the 400-year-old yew hedge – known as the elephant hedge because of the shapes that were once cut into it. It's cut once a year and yields a ton of clippings, which are collected and used as part of a chemotherapy drug. Isn't that wonderful?

The guide then took us round to one side of the house, pointing out the bedroom where Charles Dickens slept. He was a great friend of one of the Watson family and often stayed. Apparently, he wrote the book *Bleak House* based on Rockingham Castle. This was interesting to us as we lived in Bleakhouse Road in Auckland for 20 years and all the streets coming off this road were named from Dickens' books – Nickleby Place, Copperfield Terrace, Pickwick Parade, Oliver Twist Ave and Micawber Place.

After so much food over the weekend, dinner that night back at Bridget and Richard's, was poached eggs on toast. "What the hell?" Steve teased Bridget, looking aghast at his plate but giving her a wink and deliberately dropping his knife and fork, which clattered to the table. "Standards are slipping here, Annemarie. I think we'll go home in the morning."

He had a sore shoulder the next day where Bridget had clocked him one for being so cheeky!

Back in March I mentioned meeting Anne when I went to check out the B&B she ran. Well, that first time I stepped into Anne and Richard's home, I just loved the fragrance wafting through the hallway. After several visits, I finally asked Anne what it was. "Wait right there," she said, disappearing upstairs. Several minutes later she reappeared with a little package and placed it in my hands. "A little gift for you."

It was a Branche d'Olive diffuser, named Garrigue. It's described as 'a delicious citrus cologne with top notes of bergamot and citrus around aromatic lavender and thyme on a woody sandalwood base.' It's their signature scent. Take it from me, it's just divine and I loved walking into our flat and having this very same fragrance greet me when I came in the door.

As you will have gathered, Bridget and Richard go out of their way for us when we stay and I wanted to take something special with me, as a thank-you gift. Anne had told me about the lovely gift shop, Heirloom, in our High Street where I could buy the diffuser. Heirloom's owner was a delightful young woman called Emma. She was full of personality and passion for her trade. When I specifically asked for the Garrigue fragrance, a smile played on her face, and she told me I'd chosen the best fragrance in her shop.

"Did you know that it's Chef Raymond Blanc's favourite room fragrance? He has it in every suite of his beautiful hotel in Oxford, called *Le Manoir aux Quat'Saisons*?"

"No, I didn't. I love Raymond Blanc, his food and TV shows," I replied. "What a nice little story."

"Ah," she said, pointing her finger at the wall, "did you also know that Raymond Blanc's UK headquarters is right next door, on the other side of this wall?"

My jaw dropped and I stared at her a little unbelievingly, stepping back out onto the street to take a closer look at next door. Steve and I had often wondered what was behind the mirrored windows, presuming it to be a private club. I moved back inside.

"Behind that door with its brass plaque, is a team of thirty people. All working in their allotted cubicles in a huge room, painted a beautiful, calming bluey-grey, and running Raymond's little empire," Emma proudly informed me. "He loves Teddington and is often here for meetings over there," she pointed to The Kings Head, "but I've actually never seen him."

When The Kings Head came up for sale, Raymond Blanc snapped it up and it's now one of his many White Brasserie chain of restaurants. Steve and I had lunch there with Mary and Symon, one Sunday back in May. The food, ambiance and staff were very good.

"Most days," Emma continued, "I watch the staff from next door trotting across the road during lunchtime, returning with a covered plate of something wonderful from the pub kitchen while I'm stood here munching on my M&S sandwich! Something's not right there," she laughed.

With my beautifully wrapped package tucked in my handbag, I hurried home to Google *Le Manoir aux Quat'Saisons* and, *Ooh la la*, what a gorgeous place, with its sumptuous rooms, gardens, dinners and cookery courses. I couldn't wait to relay all of this to Bridget (a wondrous cook and *pâtissier*) when I handed over our little Garrigue diffuser gift. I thought she and Richard would just love to go there.

Once Steve had dropped our bags in our room and the kettle was on, I produced the gift with a little flourish and gave it to Bridget, relaying its back story. Bridget stood smiling politely and waited patiently until I'd finished telling her all about Chef Raymond Blanc and *Le Manoir aux Quat'Saisons*. "This looks gorgeous. Thank you both very much," she hugged us "but I have to tell you that Richard and I *have* actually stayed at *Le Manoir*." You could have knocked me down with a feather.

She explained: "When Richard retired, he was given a farewell gift of a cookery course at *Le Manoir aux Quat'Saisons*. As soon as I discovered this, I promptly got on the Internet and booked us in for dinner and to stay the night. Well, I would have been stupid not to. It has such a fabulous reputation and I do have to say, it was the most incredible dinner and beautiful place to stay." Bridget was almost misty-eyed, remembering that time and, behind her, Richard nodded in confirmation.

"The best part of the whole experience was when Raymond Blanc himself sat down at our table and started chatting with us. He was just so charming and seemingly genuine. It was wonderful," she said.

I was so envious of their good fortune. I looked forward to the day when I walked up our High Street and saw Raymond walking towards me. What would I say to him? *Bonjour* of course, and kiss him on both cheeks ...

One glorious Sunday started with an early morning walk along the Thames Path from Teddington Lock through to Kingston for coffee, a croissant, and a few groceries. With brilliant blue skies and a warming sun, the day was full of promise.

Anglers were parked on camping chairs at various points along the riverbank, their camouflage jackets buttoned to the neck and caps pulled low, twitching their lines, waiting for that elusive nibble on the bait. Some of their kit was impressive – fold-up boxes with many slots for the assorted items of tackle, sandwiches and filled thermos at the ready too. Some must camp out for the night as there were sleeping bags. It was a very serious business. Several had two or three rods set a little distance apart. I never did see anyone catch anything and to be honest, I don't think I'd like to eat anything out of the Thames ...

Lots of runners and dog walkers were out with us too and it seemed that we said good morning every few steps, it was that busy. Everyone was relishing the start of the day and the glorious sunshine.

Some of the magnificent houses on the other side of the river had lush lawns running down to a jetty or pier, where a boat of some sort was moored. Often we saw a couple having breakfast at one of these homes, sitting on their lovely terrace and soaking up the morning sun and we'd wave to each other.

A regatta was getting underway at the boating club and little white sails, hoisted up the rigging, were buffeted by a gentle breeze. Further on, rowers ploughed their way through the water, the coxswain shouting and driving them to strive harder. Houseboats, swans, geese and ducks bobbed up and down as motor craft puttered by, but the birdlife seemed oblivious to it all, cruising serenely on the ripples, upstream to the gaggle-gathering point on the other side of Kingston Bridge. They knew there was always someone there with a bag of something for them.

Often on our early morning walks, no matter what the season or temperature, we'd come across a serious group of swimmers who'd strip down to their bathers, pull on a cap, a fluorescent red 'floater' onto their back and stride into the freezing cold water. Some did wear wetsuits. I shivered just watching them but gave a cherry hello as we passed, dressed in our jackets, gloves and beanies. I thought them quite mad, and I would certainly never have put my face into that water. Yuck. Wearing a floater was necessary in order to be seen by boaters and not get run over.

Our morning coffee and shopping completed, we retraced our steps back along the path home to shower and get ourselves suitably attired to attend the Concours d'Elegance at Hampton Court Palace. This is a spectacular event, showcasing many of the rarest cars from around the world, and we'd been given tickets to attend.

I'm no car enthusiast but couldn't help but be impressed with the exquisite cars on display in such an elegant setting. These ranged from shooting brakes to the latest high-performance sports cars in metallic orange or shimmering greens. Proud owners stood beside their cars, bonnets up, espousing the qualities and engine capabilities. Most of it went over our heads and after a tour of all the cars we followed a worn track to the champagne tent and food trucks.

Seated at an outdoor table and out of the glaring sun under a red and white striped umbrella, we tucked into delicate egg and cress club sandwiches and delightful smoked salmon blinis — perfect for the occasion and accompanied by a glass of Taittinger. I was as happy as a sandboy, people-watching and sipping that seductive champagne.

A couple arrived and asked to share our table, which we of course agreed to with alacrity. Here was someone new to chat to and I was always open to that ... What lovely people. We passed a very pleasant hour, exchanged phone numbers, and set a date for a walk and a coffee in a few weeks time. Perfect.

August Snippets

French tarts. Anne (from Anne and Bruce) was keen to join a French class and asked me if I'd like to go and start learning again. Knowing we'd be back and forth to France while we were living in Teddington, I thought it a good idea. The class was within walking distance for me, but if the weather was mucky, Anne kindly picked me up. Silvie was our talented teacher, French born and equally as eloquent in English. I completed several terms of French but it was all getting too hard with the tenses and verbs and conjugations. My head hurt, so I stopped.

But what came out of that class were fabulous friendships with two other women, Jacqui and Izzy, both of whom were English.

Jacqui had a fabulous life, part of which was frequently trekking back and forth to Monaco where her daughter, son-in-law and two granddaughters lived, and Izzy owned a second home in Antibes, often going out there to sort out this and that or just have some well-earned R&R from her hectic life.

I named us The French Tarts and we'd meet once a month for coffee at a gorgeous café in our High Street actually named The French Tarte! The four of us shared many stories and laughter. Lucky me – once again.

The Summer Exhibition, Royal Academy, London. This fabulous exhibition has been held every year since 1769 and displays the weird and whacky as well as mainstream art (in all its forms) from established and emerging artists. Every wall is alive, covered with canvasses, photographs and small sculptures, with the bigger pieces perched on a plinth or box on the floor. Steve and I wandered for several hours with Anne and Richard, sipping a glass of champagne and taking it all in. Just marvellous to see such disparate groupings of creativity.

The following link will take you directly to photos associated with August. Feel free to comment on any of them.

https://bit.ly/LLA_August-2018

SEPTEMBER 2018

What a month. It all started with the most magical ten days in Spain with Auckland friends, Ann and Kevin. Somehow Kevin manages to find perfect accommodation. He must scour the Internet for hours as, on previous holidays and when travelling through France together, he'd picked some stunning places. It was no different for Spain. Earlier in the year, Kevin had Skyped us: "So, we've mapped out a bit of a plan, starting in Granada and finishing in Seville," he said, showing us the route on his map. "Is there anywhere in particular that you want to go?"

"Nope, just very happy to do whatever you want to do, as the only part of Spain we've been to is Barcelona," Steve told him.

"Oh, okay. Well, do you want to see the accommodation I'm proposing? I'm very happy to look at alternatives," Kevin offered kindly.

"Nope, we know your selections will be perfectly nice and we're very happy to leave it to you. Just tell us what we owe you, send us your bank details and we'll deposit the funds. Honestly, we are so appreciative you have done all the homework and hard work," I told him.

And that's what happened. I was thrilled. It was the easiest holiday I've ever had to arrange ...

Our meet-up city was Granada – home to the historic and stunning Alhambra Palace and Gardens and fabulous little streets filled with people, music, enticing tapas bars and restaurants. Our cute apartment was above the intersection of four of these very streets and we stepped outside our front door, straight into the hustle and bustle and colour of Spanish life.

In one beautiful, old traditional bar, tiled in the most gorgeous colourful tiles depicting country life, the barman brought the gin bottle and tonic to the table, to pour the drinks in front of Ann and me. As he lifted the gin bottle and proceeded to pour, I think he was waiting for us to say 'when' but we both stayed silent ... Those two gin and tonics could strip wallpaper, they were that strong! Fabulous though.

Aged and pungent Serrano and Iberian hams hung from the ceiling in so many of these tapas bars, alongside bunches of deep red chillies. We were all salivating at the aroma of these and the bar snacks on offer. Every drink was accompanied by a little tasty something and all part of the price. Who needed dinner?

The next day, in the cool of the morning, we set off to explore the wondrous Alhambra. Not only a palace but a fortress built by the Emir Muslims in a blend of medieval Islamic, Moorish and Christian architecture. The complex is made up of palaces, courtyards, fountains and gardens. Everything is a work of art – the intricate carvings, vividly coloured tiles, arches and geometric patterns. It is such a vast property that it takes hours to walk and to take it all in. In the sultry evening air we hiked to a lookout point across the valley from the Palace to see it against the backdrop of the Sierra

Nevada peaks and back-lit with soft lights, illuminating the stonework and the magnificent garden. It truly was a magical place.

Dipping in and out of the stores the next day, Ann and I had fun pretending we were discerning *señoras*, mucking about with flamenco dresses and well hidden from possible frosty looks from the shop assistant. Deciding we couldn't quite pull off the look we hung them back on the rack, making a hasty, giggling exit out the door.

Our next stop on Kevin's Magical Tour of Spain was Ronda – in Malaga and inland from the Costa del Sol. Again, our beautiful and traditional apartment was situated in the heart of the town, above a busy pedestrianised shopping street. During siesta time though, you could have fired a gun down the street; there wasn't a soul about. In the warmth of the evening, Ann and I were very content to watch the steady stream of shoppers and restaurant-goers pass by, while we chatted on the balcony, sipping a glass of wine before we all went in search of our own dinner.

In Ronda we discovered a satisfying and refreshing drink called tinto de verano – consisting of red wine and lemon soda. It was the perfect accompaniment to hot Spanish weather and Ann and I drank plenty of it. Imagine our delight when in a supermarket we found it in two-litre bottles – just like Coke or Fanta. It was so much cheaper too, so several bottles were stashed in the trolley.

Ronda is now one of my favourite Spanish towns. The landscape is incredibly dramatic and breathtaking. It's famous for the bridge, Puente Nuevo, which spans a vertiginous gorge and plunges nearly 400 feet down to the river, right in the middle of town. The bridge took 34 years to build, starting in 1759. A chamber above the central arch was used as a prison. During the 1936–1939 Civil War both sides allegedly used the prison as a torture chamber for captured opponents, killing some by throwing them from the windows to the rocks at the bottom of the El Tajo gorge. Horrific.

The four of us walked the steep zigzag down to the water's edge, just to crane our necks and look up at this magnificent feat of engineering.

Another captivating part of Ronda is Alameda del Tajo, a beautiful park with a wide, paved and tree-lined avenue which leads out to exceptional views of the gorge. The advice is not to lean too far over the wrought-iron railing as it's dizzying looking down to the deep ravine and houses below. The park is a cool haven in which to rest from the heat, away from the bustle of the restaurants and cafés, and sit and listen to classical musicians or watch artists creating landscapes on their canvases.

The food on offer in Ronda was so tantalising. Café windows were stuffed full of ham and cheese rolls, meat sandwiches encased in folds of pastry and paper cones filled with spicy little sausage bites, or a local cheese. It was all so mouth-watering. But it didn't stop there. Further down the street we stood drooling outside the bakery where works of art, in the form of round chocolate cases filled with delicate, creamy custard, topped with glistening fruits, sat nestled up against lemon tarts, pastries and other tempting cakes. What was the point of resisting? We pushed the door open and succumbed to the heavenly delights within, closing our eyes and inhaling the sweet fragrances while waiting in line.

The elegant town of Jerez welcomed us next. The architecture, building façades, statuary, gardens and fountains were stunning. Kevin deliberately mapped our trip to include Jerez as it's the birthplace (1835) of Tio Pepe sherry. He'd already bought tickets for a tour and tasting at the famous Bodegas González Byass.

A bottle of Tio Pepe is very distinctive and the name and company logo have been humanised by a man wearing a wide-brimmed red hat, a red Andalucían jacket and holding a guitar by its neck. It is everywhere, and Kevin decided he needed to create a Tio Pepe call and drove me batty, hollering every time we came across a Tio Pepe man, 'Hey, T-i-o P-e-p-e'! in a loud, accented sing-song voice, causing people to stop and grin at him. Honestly, I think he'd swallowed too many of the tastings. It was very funny.

Regardless of whether you drink alcohol or not, when in Jerez, go on a tour of Bodegas González Byass. It's the most beautiful winery, set in the wine-making centre of Constancia. Whitewashed buildings, dressed in vibrant pink bougainvillea vines or deep green ivy abound, with archways leading into the cool of the cellars and wine tasting areas. These were incredibly modern, made of steel and glass and a great juxtaposition with the old. It's easy to pass an hour happily wandering through the little streets, shaded from the dazzling sunlight by the entwined vines, which run across overhead wires connecting one rooftop with another. The formal garden is also a delight.

A miniature red train provides transport between the ancient cellars where it's fabled that 'drunken mice climb tiny step ladders, put in place by thoughtful members of staff, to sip sweet Pedro Ximénez from traditional sherry glasses'. I was looking out for these mice but funnily enough, never did see any.

The ethos of the company is: *Tío Pepe is more than a wine – it's a mood, an attitude towards life.* It really is a magical and timeless place to visit, and it seems impossible to leave without buying a bottle of something. Kevin bought several...

Our hosts at our elegant Jerez apartment welcomed us in with drinks in the garden. Kevin had outdone himself again, in choosing this place. Entry was via a set of high, black wrought-iron gates, crossing an internal tiled foyer and in through a timbered front door. The foyer was beautifully furnished with a pendulous chandelier, a centred, glossy mahogany round table and framed prints on the walls. A timbered staircase led to the upper apartments and an internal balcony ran around the interior on two levels. With a glass of cool wine in hand, we sat out under the trees by the pool, chatting and reflecting on our trip. The water was so refreshing, and the heat of the day washed away as we floated and drifted until it was time to shower and wander into town for dinner.

The seaside town of Cádiz is only a half hour out of Jerez and it was another fabulous day, gate-crashing a wedding and exploring the fortress and historic buildings around the waterfront.

The gate-crashing came first. We'd just got out of the car when a flash of colour caught my eye. A beautifully gowned woman went up the steps and into a nearby church. Soon others were going in and I could hear the strains of organ music. With my nosy reputation and name of Detective Inspector Rawson, I just had to go and investigate. "Quick, Ann." I caught her by the wrist, pulling her along behind me. "Let's go and see what's happening. Look, there's another woman looking very gorgeous going in. Oh, and look at those sweet children!"

We arrived at the church door just in time to see the most beautiful Spanish bride and her proud father step out of a sleek black Mercedes. Her glossy, mahogany-black hair had been twisted up and into a knot, holding a short and simple cream veil, while the most lustrous, creamy-white gown fell in perfect folds from her slim hips. She couldn't stop smiling, flashing perfect white teeth.

The female guests' outfits were a riot of colour – one a glorious teal-coloured, wide-legged jumpsuit, splashed with vivid cerise-pink flowers and cut low at the back. She had donned a glamorous wide-brimmed, teal straw hat and finished her outfit with a cerise-pink band. Another was in a baby-blue, tulle-skirted dress with a wide, gold silk band tied around her waist, perfectly matched with baby blue pumps and a flamboyantly decorated gold straw hat. Just inside the door was yet another elegant and beautiful woman, decked out in a halter- neck 'enchanted garden'. The white background of her floor-length dress was a mass of large red, pink, green and blue flowers. It was glorious and she happily posed for me so I could snap her, with the heavily embellished gold altar and lustrous floor-to-ceiling reliefs as her background. Where did all these beautiful women come from?

To the spine-tingling strains of the organ and the soprano soloist, the bride and her father began their slow journey down the aisle to her waiting fiancé. Ooh, I do love a wedding and this one looked to be incredible. Imagine what the food must have been like.

"Hurry up you two! Stop drooling and catch up." Kevin beckoned us on. He and Steve were already halfway down the street, not at all interested in the frocks and proceedings.

"Men." Ann rolled her eyes at me as we scooted up the street. "They just don't get it do they?"

Markets are high on the lists of all four of us and the fish market at Cádiz is one of the best we've ever seen. Every type of fish and shellfish from the nearby waters was for sale. The vendors shouted their wares, trying to induce the many locals getting their daily bits and bobs to buy their seafood. The fruit and vegetable market was bursting with colour, variety and style, creating a visual feast. The distinctive fragrance of the fat and luscious black figs was just too much. I had to buy some for our entrée at home that night. All this deliciousness was making us hungry, and I could see Steve looking at his watch, wondering if it was too early for lunch.

"Kevin, the sun's over the yardarm, fancy a beer?" Steve asked. "And I'm starving, can we eat?"

"Yep, I'm in. It's getting too hot to wander for much longer.

Let's head back into the town and find somewhere cool for lunch and that beer," Kevin replied. "You girls ready?"

Ann and I were starting to wilt in the heat, and I was most definitely ready for my daily dose of tinto de verano. "Yes!" we chorused, moving up beside them.

Sizzling, garlicky prawns and charred, green padron peppers arrived for us to share while we dived into our refreshing drinks and decided on our mains. It was all fish on the menu, but when in Cádiz ...

The following day was set aside to visit The White Villages of Andalucía – Arcos, Grazalema and Zahara. From Jerez our first stop at Arcos was only 45 minutes away. After parking on the outskirts we climbed to see the castle and an incredible view from a sprawling plaza at the top of the village. The hillside, covered in scrub, fell deeply and sharply away beneath us, down to the tree-lined, winding river. We could see for miles into the distance.

A falconer was in the plaza with an army of birds in a large cage – mainly hawks of various kinds, but several owls too. For a fee, you could have your photo taken with one of these perched on your arm. None of us did.

Wandering through the village we came across a souvenir shop, selling the usual Spanish ceramics, key rings and place mats. Ann spied a row of vivid red and black polka dotted, frilled and flouncy dresses towards the back of the shop. She was on a mission, making a beeline for them.

"Get a photo of this, Annemarie." Ann pulled one of the dresses off the rack and draped it across her body, placing her hand on one hip, showing it off in style. I quickly snapped her and grabbed another style, adopting the same pose.

"The Howick girls will be green with envy, when I walk into coffee wearing this," Ann smirked. Visualising that very picture, we were both in fits of giggles. Not wanting to be offensive to the shop owner we managed to contain our mirth, but it all got a bit much when we caught Kevin and Steve gaping in horror through the window. We quickly put the dresses back, called a quick '*gracias*' and hurried out of the shop, bursting out laughing when we came face-to-face with the guys. Like silly schoolgirls, we were. Honestly.

On we drove to Grazalema in search of lunch but, after a fruitless hunt for a car park, Kevin pushed on to Zahara, expertly manoeuvring us through some hair-raising chicanes and managing to avoid the lunatics crossing the middle line, coming the other way. It wasn't just Steve who was starving by the time we installed ourselves in a tiny restaurant, gazing hungrily at the menu.

In case you were interested, the reason why a lot of villages in Spain are white is to protect the houses from the sun during summer. This helps to keep the homes cooler during the intense summer heat as the white colour reflects sunlight, rather than absorbing it. This little bit of wisdom originates from the Moors.

Next stop – Seville. Wow! Spain is such a stunning country. I'd fallen in love with the architecture, the parks and open spaces and the wonderful food and wine – and Seville delivered.

Kevin's apartment of choice in Seville was yet another delight – traditional and beautifully fitted out, with a full kitchen, relaxing sitting room and the cutest balcony for Ann and me to perch on, enjoying our wine and the fabulous scenarios playing out beneath us. Our Seville home sat above the orange tree-lined square of Plaza de la Contratación, on the route of the Seville horse carriage rides. From our prime position we could watch them clip-clop their way around with their many and varied passengers, waving to them and raising our glasses as they passed by.

On our last day in Seville the four of us climbed aboard our own carriage for a tour. It was such a different thing for us to do as we're usually on foot. I felt like royalty in that carriage and had my hand poised, mid-air, just like a Queen, ready to wave to all and sundry as we passed by. However, I had a deep concern for the horses. They appeared well looked after, watered and fed and I was told they were rested in the shade during the worst of the heat, and we did witness that from our vantage point on the balcony.

Our accommodation was perfectly positioned to visit Seville Cathedral, just around the corner. We joined the relatively short queue half an hour before opening time. The sheer wealth, immensity of size and detailing in the vast cathedral was overwhelming. It was cavernous and humbling all at the same time and hard to take it all in. It was just the same at the Church of El Salvador. Gold, gold, gold and more gold, dazzling on the eye and absolutely jaw-dropping. So much money was poured into these places. For the glory of God? Or for the glory of the already rich kings, queens and religious orders? Meanwhile, the hungry lined the streets and died in the gutters ... Enough! On to happier chat.

The classically beautiful Alcazar Palace and Gardens, the royal palace for the Christian King Peter of Castile (only once they had destroyed an Abbasid Muslim residential fortress after their conquest of Seville) was nearby too and a 'must see' on our itinerary. The architecture, decorations, colour and style are mainly Muslim rather than Christian and the continuous, perfectly formed archways created squares around the lush, tranquil and manicured gardens. Low fountains, gently tinkling, created a sense of calm and wellbeing. The age and beauty of these places is mind-blowing at times, as is the deeply rooted history.

On a day trip from Seville to Córdoba we toured the Mezquita de Córdoba – the central Mosque Cathedral. 'It's impossible to overemphasise the beauty of Córdoba's great mosque, with its remarkably serene and spacious interior. One of the world's greatest works of Islamic architecture, the Mezquita hints, with all its lustrous decoration, at a refined age when Muslims, Jews and Christians lived side by side and enriched their city with a heady interaction of diverse, vibrant cultures.' Thank you, *Lonely Planet*. This describes the place perfectly. Astonishingly, the Cathedral took 250 years to complete.

All too soon our Spanish adventure came to an end. What a fun-filled and relaxing touring holiday with Ann and Kevin. They continued on to Lisbon and we boarded a flight for London.

Steve and I were due back at work, and I needed to gear up for a royal visit. Well, she's nearly royalty. She's my younger sister, Jill and her husband, Ferg. Ferg had business meetings booked in London but, with their youngest daughter, Victoria, moving to London not long after us, it was a bonus for them to spend time with her as well as us. I knew there'd be fun and mischief during Jill's stay in London and I wasn't disappointed.

"Hi mum, it's me. Are you home the weekend after next? I'm coming over to play golf. Can I crash on your couch for a couple of nights please?" It was Cam (Campbell), our eldest son who lived in Adelaide, on the phone. He was a professional golfer and usually played tournaments in China, but he'd seen one he qualified for in England and decided it would be a great opportunity to catch up with us.

"What? Really? You're coming here? Oh, Cam, that'd be fantastic. Oh, I can't wait to see you. Steve! It's Cam. He's coming over for a tournament and will stay with us here for a couple of nights. Oh, this is so exciting! We'll have to get Murdoch over too. Steve, Cam's coming."

"Mum, mum, calm down will you and listen," Cam laughed.

He was always moderate and wasn't one to leap up and down – unlike his excitable mother. Steve jumped on the bandwagon too.

"Annemarie, calm down and listen to what Cam's saying." The men in my family don't show a lot of emotion … how did they end up being my husband and sons?

"Yes, mum, I've already spoken to Murdoch. He's around and wants us to go over to Brixton and have lunch so I can see where he lives. I'll leave you to sort that with him – and dinner at yours one night, if he can. I'll also be back for two nights at the end of the tournament. I've got to fly but I'll be hiring a car at Heathrow and will email you all the details. Love you." And with that final note, he was gone, and I was left staring at my phone.

My mind was furiously working overtime and, when I looked at the calendar, Cam's last two nights with us were going to coincide with Jill and Ferg's visit. "Oh my God, Steve, Jill and Ferg are here at the same time as Cam. We could have them *all* here for dinner, Murdoch and Victoria included."

"That's a good idea. You'd better see if they can all make it then, knowing the kids' social lives and that Jill and Ferg might have business dinners. I'll let you sort it out." And with that Steve returned to his book.

Meanwhile, I got tapping on the phone, getting in touch with everyone, but then stopped mid-message. "Hey, I've got a brilliant idea. Listen, Steve." I waited until his head was out of the book and he was looking at me. "Why don't we have a restaurant lunch out with everyone, and we can make it our family Christmas? I can get Christmas crackers for the table, some little Christmassy ornaments and make it special."

That was me gone – inside my head, busy planning it all and I only caught murmurings from the sofa. I guessed Steve said yes.

Two days later all was arranged. Everyone could make it

and I'd booked the restaurant and they (the restaurant) were perfectly happy for me to arrive early to decorate the table. It was going to be my surprise on the day.

Flowers for Mrs Harris, a wonderful book by Paul Gallico and now a play, was on at the Chichester Festival Theatre and, having loved the story, I booked us to travel down and see it. It's all about a London (Cockney) charlady and her great desire for a Dior dress, saving madly and culminating in a visit to Paris to buy it. It's such a beautiful story and the play interpreted it superbly. I was totally engrossed from start to finish, even crying at the end. It was subsequently made into a film called *Mrs Harris Goes to Paris*, starring Lesley Manville, whom I very much admire. At the time of writing this, the film came to our village. It was brilliant and I cried all over again.

It was raining cats and dogs and cold when we left the theatre, so it was a mad dash for the train back to London, leaping over sloshy puddles on the way. Believe me, the entertainment was just as good on the train as at the theatre. Three young women, all clones of each other – long bottle-blonde hair, false eyelashes, caked-on make-up and wearing very little clothing – were lounging in the doorway, struggling to keep their huge suitcases from rolling down the aisle, but managing to keep up inane, loud chit-chat, with a lot of hair flicking and eye-rolling to boot.

In our full carriage people were catching each other's eye and pretending not to hear the girls' conversation. It was actually impossible not to hear it and smiles played on everyone's lips. One of these girls found a seat halfway down the carriage and continued a loud conversation with the other two, still in the doorway. She then beckoned one of her buddies to join her, nudging the innocuous little man next to her.

"You're a'right, ain't cha. Ya don't mind squeezing up a bit so me girlfriends can come and sit 'ere?" she said, almost battering him to death with her false eyelashes.

The poor man blushed to the roots of his hair, struggling not to notice the fleshy breasts spilling over the skin-tight top next to him and stammered, "Oh, oh, oh, no. Um, that's fine, yes." He then pressed himself up against the window, trying to avoid the large, squishy thigh touching his.

That was the end, and everyone burst out laughing, including the three girls. It was all done good-naturedly, and no one was being offensive or offended.

Not just one but the three of them managed to squish in together. Out came a bottle of fizz, the top popped off and it was passed from one to the other with them all drinking straight from the bottle. I was fascinated and couldn't take my eyes off them. They were so busy talking ten-to-the-dozen and sharing this bottle of wine, they nearly missed their Gatwick Airport stop.

A shriek went up when they realised the doors would be closing any minute. It was a mad scramble to get their suitcases to the door and onto the platform. They made it! Guess where they were going? Ibiza. Who'd have known? They were great fun and just enjoying themselves, absolutely no bother, but definitely entertaining.

Back in Teddington, the change in the air was evident. The leaves were turning from a dull, summer-dried green into golds, russets and chocolate brown and creating multi-coloured, thick carpets everywhere. On our bench next door, we made the most of the late afternoon, having a glass of wine before dinner, watching the paddle-boarders and small boats pootling around on the water. One paddle-boarder had his dog, happily dozing in the sun on one end, as he desultorily spooned his way under the bridge. Across the water, it was almost a highway, with so many people on the Thames Path walking, biking or running in the tepid sunshine.

A great indicator of autumn and winter's impending arrival were the flocks of geese, flying over in the evenings in V formation with the leader honking loudly, keeping the rest on course, flying in from the north to settle in the UK (surprisingly) for winter.

"We're here! I'm shattered and the bags under my eyes are enormous, but we need to keep going. Are you coming in to see us?" It was 11.00 a.m. and Jill and Ferg had arrived at their central London hotel.

"Of course! I'm thrilled to bits you're here. I'll be there in an hour. See you soon. We'll do a big walk to wake you up," I said.

"I'm that woozy, but we'll pop out for a bite to eat and meet you out the front of the hotel. A walk will be great. I'm so looking forward to seeing you." I could hear the tiredness in Jill's voice. They'd completed a marathon 30 hours from New Zealand to London with minimal sleep and were having four nights in town while Ferg got his business stuff out of the way.

The Sunday morning of our September Christmas lunch was freezing cold. It felt like winter was with us already, but I didn't care about the weather. I was so excited, knowing our family and Jill and Ferg and their daughter Victoria were all getting together. I had it all planned out. During the week a friend had driven me to Squires in Twickenham to buy Christmas crackers and festive decorations and, as soon as I got home, I'd hastily hidden them in the back of the wardrobe.

"I'll see you both at the restaurant. I'm catching an earlier train as I've got a couple of things to do on my way," I told Cam and Steve, pulling on my coat and scarf. Cam had returned to us for his last two nights in the UK.

"Oh, Okay." Steve looked at me quizzically, no doubt

wondering what on earth I could possibly need to get as we were eating lunch out and certainly wouldn't need dinner. He'd understand once he got to the restaurant and saw the table festively decorated.

I quickly snuck into our bedroom, pulled my bag of tricks out from the back of the wardrobe and hurried to the front door, not wanting to be seen. "See you soon!" I yelled, pulling the door behind me. I heard their muffled response as I hurried down the stairs.

It was that bitter, I sat in the waiting room at Teddington station to keep out of the wind, placing my carry bag on the floor beside me. Caught in conversation with the man next to me I didn't hear the train and, seeing it arriving at the platform through the window, he and I quickly jumped up to get on.

It wasn't until the train pulled into Waterloo station and I bent down to scoop up my bag of decorations that I realised I'd left it in the waiting room, back at Teddington. I was that upset! There wasn't time to go back and get them. Totally annoyed with myself for being so stupid, and feeling miserable that it was just going to be an ordinary lunch, I made my way to the restaurant. I was the first there of course and explained my stupidity to the *maitre'd*, who was kind and sympathetic.

"Crazy I know, but you wouldn't happen to have any Christmas decorations stored away, would you?" I asked him in desperation and hope.

"Oh I am so sorry but everything is boxed up and kept off site. There's no room for storage here. I wish I could help you. Let me get you a drink, while you wait for the others to arrive."

I was sitting, twiddling my wine glass round and round, when Steve and Cam came through the door. I burst into tears.

"What on earth's happened, mum?" Cam took me by the arm.

"Oh, I had these lovely plans to surprise everyone, making the table so Christmassy with decorations and crackers," I blubbed. "I'd even hidden them so you wouldn't know what I was up to. That's why I left home early." Both quickly glanced at the table, noting there were no decorations. "And I stupidly left them in the waiting room at Teddington station!" I wailed. "I wanted it to be so special."

Cam was patting my arm and Steve was rubbing my shoulder, when the others burst through the door, full of life and chatter. Jill stopped in her tracks, seeing that I was upset. Cam quickly explained. Everyone reassured me it was a wonderful idea but that it didn't matter in the slightest, because wasn't it great that we could all just be together? Of course it was. That's all that really mattered.

After welcoming hugs and kisses all round, Steve ordered drinks and our Christmas lunch was under way. It was fabulous.

On our way home I called into the ticket office at Teddington station, just on the off chance that someone might have found my bag and handed it in. Sure enough, it had been, and I was doubly delighted because I'd put a very nice pair of black patent leather shoes in there, ready for me to slip into at the restaurant. A very kind and honest man had handed it in, proving there are good people out there.

Jill and Ferg were still in town at this stage, so the next morning, while Ferg and Steve were beavering away at work, Jill and I made the most of sister time and met for coffee and a muffin before a full day out and about. We had so much fun and I'm grinning like a twit, about to recount our shenanigans.

We both love the upmarket department store, Fortnum & Mason, and after being graciously swept through the front doors by the top-hatted doorman, we floated around the floors, playing at being ladies and enjoying the luxury oozing from every shelf and display. A stand of ridiculously adorned and ridiculously priced (£45) white shower caps – some with plastic strawberries or yellow and red dahlias stuck on, others with stitched colourful bows – were too hard for Jill to resist. She quickly grabbed one, plonked it on, turned this way and that, admiring herself in the mirror, both of us in fits of giggles. I found a fabulous black fedora, with a thin black leather band, tilted it on my head at a rakish angle and proceeded to prance around the hat aisle, my arm outstretched holding an invisible lead and pretending I was out walking my beautifully coiffed poodle in Hyde Park. Where were the shop assistants to reprimand us?

Next it was on to the china displays. Beautiful striped cups and saucers in many different colours sat next to matching teapots, sugar bowls and milk jugs. One table had a magnificent display of oriental teas, each one set into a portico in a miniature Taj Mahal, complete with ornate and studded 'onion' domes. Floral cups and saucers and teapots, matching the tea caddy, were strategically placed too. I nearly died when Jill put her hand into one portico, picked up a cup and saucer and proceeded to pretend to drink from it! Any minute now, I was sure we would be tapped on the shoulder, grabbed by the scruff of our necks and propelled towards the door. It didn't happen but we quickly scooted out of the shop, still laughing at our silly antics, halfway up the street.

At a brisk pace we moved on to spend an hour in the National Portrait Gallery before sitting down to a delightful lunch and a glass of rosé, talking our heads off, at the North Audley Cantine, a classy little French restaurant in Mayfair offering sharing plates and divine desserts.

With full tummies, Jill and I tottered our way through more of luxurious Mayfair, into Hyde Park then Green Park before arriving in Piccadilly to meet up with the lovely Tom and Margo, down from Glasgow, to have a wee drink with them. By this stage Jill was moaning. There's a family joke about my little sister 'never being 100 per cent'. This time she had a sore toe, from all our walking. There's always something not quite right ... but I still love her.

September ended with a jaunt out to Windsor and Eton. I'd been to Windsor as a young woman of 22 but didn't remember it, at all – apart from the castle of course. And there it was, in all its historic glory of round towers, thick, grey-stone walls and many crenellations.

Steve and I had deliberately caught an early train on the Sunday morning, arriving in Windsor around 9.30 a.m., wanting to avoid the weekend crowds. In less than an hour, busloads of tourists had disgorged and the queue to the castle gate snaked down the road, making it difficult to get up the main street.

From the rear castle gates and on the historic Long Walk you can soak up the history, almost seeping out of the castle walls, when you turn and look up at the awe-inspiring views. Deer roamed free, foraging in amongst the ancient oak trees.

The town of Windsor is so pretty. Our rambles took us into the heart of the shopping precinct and I did a double-take, passing the window of Madame Posh, a luxurious tearoom. Framed in the centre of it was a finely detailed, cream-coloured wedding gown, covered in intricate flowers and with a frill around the bottom – all entirely edible and made of icing; a magical work of art that would have taken weeks to complete.

Inside, customers sipping tea and coffee were cushioned in gloriously floral and upholstered wingback armchairs, placed under twinkling glass chandeliers in front of a cream-painted, ornate fireplace. Vases filled with huge bunches of sumptuous red and white roses sat on the countertops of cabinets stuffed with hunger-inducing sandwiches and cakes. Everything was reflected in, and bounced round the room, by the enormous, scrolled mirror hanging above the fireplace.

"We better not go in, Steve." I caught his arm as he was about the push the door open.

He looked at me in surprise. "Why ever not? This is right up your alley."

"You'll never get me out of that armchair. It's all so beautiful and I'd just want to cosy in and never leave."

Steve just snorted and pushed me inside. "Just your usual?" he asked. I nodded and made a beeline for an empty table and two of those squishy, inviting armchairs.

Back out on the street, a crowd had gathered around a large stall. Carluccio's had set up under a black and white striped awning. Carluccio's is a major restaurant chain, and they were celebrating a *festa dei funghi*, promoting and selling all things mushroom.

Laid out in boxes and in big round earthenware bowls were many varieties of dried porcini and fresh mushrooms and the air was thick with a deep, rich earthy aroma. Jars of porcini sauce and small tubs of mushroom and truffle paste were stacked high, in amongst tantalising oils, pastas and red wine.

A table groaned under the weight of plates and trays full of cooked strudels, tarts and arancini balls, all filled with mushrooms. It was too tempting. We grabbed a strudel and a still-warm arancini ball for our lunch, devouring them as we strolled. Just divine.

"C'mon, Eton's just down the road. Let's go for a wander to see the college." Steve wiped his mouth with a paper napkin and chewed on the last morsel of arancini.

"I've only ever seen it on TV. Right, well lead on Macduff. I guess we just follow the signposts."

It was such a lovely walk, the two of us being nosy and staring down private cobbled lanes, looking in multi-paned windows, at pretty window boxes and finding ancient stone murals on old brick walls. What a charming place. The grounds of the college cover some 1,600 acres and the collection of historic brick buildings is outstanding. It must be such a privilege to be educated within Eton's hallowed walls. Some teenage boys came out of the magnificent chapel across the road, handsomely fitted out in black frockcoat, waistcoat, pinstriped trousers and the uniform white shirt, buttoned to the neck.

"Here's some good quiz information," said Steve, his head buried in a guidebook. "Did you know that Eton has produced twenty of the UK's prime ministers? It was founded in 1440 by Henry VI. Oh, and listen to this. Currently, fees are set at £48,500 per annum. Geez, so much money!" He whistled through his teeth.

"Nope, I didn't know any of that." I was gazing through the gates, listening and looking at the statue on the other side, now realising it was Henry VI.

"No wonder it's élitist. Not too many of the run-of-the-mill income earners could afford to send dear Johnny there, that's for sure. That would actually be someone's annual income – to feed, clothe and house the children!"

"Oh, and you'll probably know this. Princes William and Harry were educated there, instead of the usual royal choice of Gordonstoun, where they would have had tutors," Steve informed me.

"Yes, I knew that about William and Harry. Much better rounding off at Eton, I would have thought. But what would I know!" I laughed.

I looked at my watch. "We'd better make tracks, Steve. We're due at Anne and Richard's at six o'clock and I need to make some sort of nibbles to take."

September Snippets

A visit to **Greenwich in London** – another fascinating and historic part of London, home to the Royal Observatory, the Royal Naval College, St Peter and Paul Chapel, Greenwich Mean Timeline and The National Maritime Museum as well as a wonderful park and lovely little township.

We'd booked the Painted Hall Ceiling Tour at the Old Royal Naval College while it was undergoing extensive renovation work. During its time, this building has been home to the Greenwich Pensioners (just like the Chelsea Pensioners), then became the Naval Officers' Mess. On this tour we climbed the scaffolding to get a close-up view of the beautiful, artistic work of Sir James Thornhill. It was difficult to get a perspective, being so close, and is vastly different from the view from the floor below.

Just imagine how difficult it was for him to paint the ceiling so that the person on the floor could see very clearly what he was creating, especially in 1707. Sir James was paid the princely sum of £1 per square yard for the walls and £3 per square yard for the ceiling. It took 19 years to complete, and the poor man wasn't paid until it was all completed.

Greenwich was humming with market shoppers and tourists. We walked back under the Thames via the tunnel from Greenwich to Canary Wharf. Such a great piece of engineering, I always think, when it allows people to walk *under* water!

Finishing up. During September, and with Steve having a full-time contract, I was able to finish my cleaning job with Anne and Bruce. Now that we were socialising together, it felt the right time to bow out and just enjoy a nice friendship. I'd still keep my two other cleaning jobs for another month but would look for different occupations now the pressure was off to bring in money quickly.

The following link will take you directly to photos associated with September. Feel free to comment on any of them.

https://bit.ly/LLA_September-2018

OCTOBER 2018
THE COTSWOLDS; THE THAMES BARRIER; SELFRIDGES

Jill and Ferg left London to tour the Lake District. We'd arranged for them to meet me off the train at Stratford-upon-Avon at the end of the week. Steve had to work, but Ferg would collect him from the train later that Friday from Moreton-in-Marsh, so we could all have a few days exploring the Cotswolds.

From Marylebone station, my train journey took me through some of England's 'green and pleasant land'. My head was twisting from window to window, enjoying the rising mist and the rich and varied autumn colours. Black-faced sheep grazed, and cows ruminated in the pastures flashing past. Helping me pass the time was a very interesting man with a Birmingham accent and a fascinating family history, from what is known as the Black Country (West Midlands). This is so named as it was once heavily industrialised and, back then, a booming part of England with coal mines, coking, iron foundries, glass factories, brickworks, and steel mills where the air was thick with soot and smoke. All hard to imagine these days. The man's grandfather and father had both died from lung conditions – just awful, but no doubt sadly common for the times.

On a brighter note, Jill, Ferg and I had a lovely couple of hours wandering around Stratford-upon-Avon, admiring the half-timbered houses with their window boxes and hanging baskets overflowing with red geraniums. Of course, we had to get a photo outside Shakespeare's house and have a walk beside the Avon, before heading to our accommodation, a very cute stone cottage called the Master's House, in Stow-on-the-Wold. It was built in the typical Cotswold stone, which comes in a range of colours. Ours was pearly coloured, with the front door and window frames painted in the softest, pale green – what I'd call a National Trust or English Heritage green. It's such a pretty colour. The cottage was brilliantly handy for the quaint shops and the essential pubs.

On our way to Stow we pulled into the town of Tetley for lunch. Tetley isn't far from Prince Charles' residence of Highgrove and has the most beautiful shop called Highgrove filled with gardening treasures and souvenir tea sets. Tickets were on sale here for a champagne high tea and garden tour of Prince Charles' place for the princely sum of £85 per person.

Our exploring wasn't dampened by the bitterly cold and rainy day. We'd come prepared for the 6 °C and the rain and went out in warm clothes, jackets and gloves, with our brollies at the ready.

The gloomy wet day didn't diminish the beauty of the Cotswold homes and buildings. Everything was so old and beautiful and mostly presented with pride. We had a lot of fun whizzing around the villages of Chipping Norton, Bourton-on-the-Water, Burford and Upper and Lower Slaughter, admiring the scenery and the cleverly constructed ancient stone walls traversing many fields. How they named some of these places intrigues me. They are so unusual. We walked narrow, twisting and turning lanes, crossed back and forth over many little bridges over the Avon and popped in and out of cute galleries and wee shops.

The warm cottage embraced us on our return and, while Jill and I poured a glass of wine and got dinner ready, the boys headed for the local pub to enjoy the ambience and a beer, even managing to catch the second half of the New Zealand v South Africa rugby match. Don't ask me who won.

The following day dawned sunny and bright, with gorgeous blue skies. Still cold but that didn't matter. I chivvied everyone through breakfast and endless cups of tea as I wanted to show them the luxurious and stylish Daylesford Farm Shop, having visited it with a cousin of mine some years earlier. I knew Jill would love it as much as I did.

At the entrance old round, zincalume tin tubs, the sort our great grandmothers were probably bathed in, were filled to overflowing with luscious herbs of every sort. Pumpkins and gourds, in varying shades of green, grey, orange, yellow and green striped, filled old farm carts, sitting beside the path leading to the front door. And inside was just as gorgeous and as sensual as I remembered it – a pungent cheese room where huge mounds of cheese sat maturing on timber shelves, a spotlessly clean meat cabinet, displaying top quality haunches and slabs of vibrant red cuts. Other cabinets were stuffed with enticing cakes, and pies and pastries were piled on the counter, just waiting to be eaten.

Freshly baked breads and free-range eggs filled chequered-cloth baskets while pastes, chutneys and local jams sat on old, washed timbered shelves. The creamery was to die for. Stunning butters, clotted creams, light cream, heavy cream, sour cream, you name it; it was in there.

Since my first visit, a floor of elegant homeware had been added, as well as shelves full of tonics and teas which looked to be locally made, and a great selection of wines. Of course, I couldn't go past the fresh and colourful vegetables, all picked from their own market garden. The whole place oozed old country charm and was just delightful. There's now also a cookery school and accommodation attached.

On Sunday night we dropped Steve at the station to return to work on Monday morning. The three of us went on to Bath for two nights, loving the town and architecture and discovering the Royal Crescent where thirty terraced houses, in the Georgian style, are set in a sweeping crescent and look out over the parkland opposite. The façade is protected I think, but owners can of course alter the inside to their taste.

From our Airbnb we could see the rear of these beautiful Georgian townhouses and it was vastly different from the uniform, tasteful frontage. Most have added a conservatory but they are a hodgepodge mix of styles. The walking tour in Bath and the one we all did in Oxford were both brilliant. They are such a great way to learn and see the history of any town. It was just such a shame Steve had to work and miss Bath.

It was time to say goodbye to Jill and Ferg. We'd so loved having time with them. Spring weather would greet them on their arrival home and new life and colour would be bursting through, just as ours was fading and falling, heading for hibernation.

With Steve working full time we needed to make the most of our weekends. He'd been wanting to go and see the Thames Barrier, the flood protection system for London and a major engineering feat.

We played the tourist on a stunning Saturday morning and caught a Thames River Cruise through Greenwich and down to the Barrier. On the journey, we listened to a very funny but also interesting commentary. Major pipe works were being undertaken on the river to replace a large section of the sewer pipes. These were originally put in to serve a population of three million people, which quickly grew to six million. Every time there was significant rain the sewer pipes didn't cope, and all the effluent would be forced out into the Thames. The new works were designed to produce a system that would resolve this and be capable of serving a growing population of perhaps ten million, with the Thames becoming much cleaner than before. The Thames was always brown as a result of the sediment and mud base being constantly churned up by all the motor craft on the river.

Over the years most of the timeworn tea and produce warehouses sitting on the Thames waterfront were replaced with luxury apartments. These waterfront homes are the most expensive real estate in London. We could see a yellow male statue in the garden of a very modern home and our captain told us this was the home of Ian McKellen, the actor. It looked a little odd amongst the old buildings.

The Thames Barrier loomed large beside us and the captain pulled back the throttle so the boat could idle while he explained how it worked. Ten steel gates can be raised into position across the River Thames, spanning some 1,700 feet. The structure protects over 30,000 acres of central London from flooding caused by tidal surges. When raised, the main gates stand as high as a five-storey building and as wide as the opening of Tower Bridge. It is such an incredible piece of engineering, saving millions of pounds worth of damage and flooding.

Once back on dry land we battled our way to the Royal Academy, through the 'Exit Brexit' march of some 760,000 people. I hung onto Steve, nervous that we'd lose sight of each other in the mêlée and noise. The Oceania Exhibition was on and anyone who took their New Zealand or Australian passport along got in free. Such a novel idea. Not many Māori works were exhibited, but what did stand out was the vivid red, highly glossed piano sculpture, on loan from the Te Papa Museum in Wellington, New Zealand. Created by New Zealander Michael Parekowhai, this piano started life as a Steinway concert grand piano, then was intricately carved in Māori motifs over a 10-year period. It is finely tuned and meant to be played. Art critics have posed the question: 'Is it a European instrument decorated with Māori carving, or a Māori carving that has engulfed a piece of European high culture?' Te Papa paid NZ$1.5M for it.

October Snippets

My friend Linley from New Zealand was in town for a few days staying at Anne's B&B, so I took her on what had become 'my tour,' through Petersham and Richmond and along the Thames Walk, knowing she would love it all too. We followed this with a fun-filled morning in the luxurious Selfridges department store, which sells anything from champagne to latex shorts. You name it, you can have it. There was the beautiful and the funky, from gorgeous shoes, glitzy boots, bags and over-the-top clothing to a modern fireplace. One man was lying back in the chair in the beauty department enjoying a full facial.

Another morning we did a tour of Ham House, which was now properly open for tourists. It was fabulous.

Sadly, Linley and Jill and Ferg were the last of the friends and family visiting the UK and Europe for that year. It would be the following summer before others arrived.

Winter draws on. The temperature in London was dropping, and the animal world was preparing for winter. I couldn't believe my eyes, seeing my first fox slinking down our driveway in broad daylight. He must have been on the hunt for food. The birds and squirrels were on a feeding frenzy, fattening themselves up ready for the winter ahead. Note to self: do *not* copy the squirrels! I'd already pulled the crock pot out from the back of the cupboard. Soup-making was on my weekend agenda, as well as stocking up on lentils and pulses for hearty winter dinners.

The word on the street was that the UK was in for a very cold winter, and light boxes and Vitamin D sprays were being advertised for those who both went to work and came home in the dark. A lot of people suffered from SAD (Seasonal Affective Disorder) syndrome over the darker months. I thought I'd just see how I coped with it all, before rushing out and buying either of those.

The following link will take you directly to photos associated with October. Feel free to comment on any of them.

https://bit.ly/LLA_October-2018

NOVEMBER 2018

TOWER OF LONDON POPPIES;
GEARING UP FOR CHRISTMAS; A
GINGERBREAD CITY AT THE V&A

'At the eleventh hour on the eleventh day of the eleventh month – we will remember them.' Armistice Day, 11 November 2018 – 100 years on.

We visited the Imperial War Museum to see the re-creation of the 2014 Tower of London installation of red ceramic poppies cascading from one of the round windows in the turret, trailing to the ground. It was named 'Blood Swept Lands and Seas of Red'. It was truly beautiful but disturbing, knowing what it represented. So many people were there, paying their solemn respects, moving quietly around the grounds, looking and remembering.

One night we took a train to the Tower of London to see the lit torches in the dry moat surrounding the tower. Lost inside our warm coats and queuing for over an hour on that cold evening, we shuffled with thousands of others to see this momentous event. It was sobering to witness ten thousand torches lit in commemoration of those lives lost. Haunting choral music filtered softly through the solemn silence shrouding us all. A beefeater, standing sentry and head bowed, was silhouetted and reflected by the flames onto a wall of the Tower, creating a looming, eerie presence.

On the morning of 11 November we joined hundreds of others in our High Street in the remembrance parade, where a lone drummer marked a beat and everyone walked in time. The parade snaked slowly, in silence, to a special service at the Cenotaph honouring all those who died in the two World Wars. All the military services were represented, as well as a few remaining veterans, seated in the front.

Each event was very emotional and caused me to remember my own father who'd fought in the Second World War. He was one of the lucky ones. He returned to his family and homeland, with the only physical evidence a scar, running from his ankle to his knee, where shrapnel was still embedded. I never did hear him speak of the war, but he must have lived with the horrors he witnessed. Sadly, he died when I was 15 so I was unable to speak to him as an adult.

In 2011, during a tour of Turkey, we'd stopped at ANZAC Cove. This is such a significant place in New Zealand and Australian war history, and one of the saddest places in the world I have ever been. The anguished and heart-wrenching inscriptions on the tombstones became blurred through my tear-filled eyes. Some of those dead were only 16 and 17, with some families losing all their sons during those bloody, horror-filled days.

"Imagine opening the door and a telegram being handed to you, telling you that your son had been killed," I said to Steve, shaking my head, trying to remove an image of receiving that news about Campbell or Murdoch.

"Horrific. Just horrific," Steve agreed.

It had been a sobering weekend, but an immensely important one for the world. Never, never can we forget the sheer number of people who died in utter misery and suffering and the lifetime of misery for those they left behind. That evening we watched a special screening on the BBC of Peter Jackson's First World War film, *They Shall Not Grow Old*. It was so well and sensitively done.

We will remember them.

It was beginning to look a lot like Christmas. Mid-November and London was lighting up magnificently. High Streets created special events to celebrate turning on their Christmas lights, pulling out all the stops, and everywhere was becoming gloriously Christmassy. It was exhilarating as this would be our first UK winter Christmas and I was hoping for snow.

I kept thinking about our visit to Munich, while we were actually living and working in France, and the fabulous Christmas markets we saw, the *glühwein* (mulled wine), the smell of sizzling *weisswurst* (white sausage) and roasting nuts, and the chalet stalls selling gorgeous decorations and gifts. And the elegant department stores and men and women on the streets. All these melded with the cold and snow, creating an absolutely magical experience. We couldn't help but get caught up in the hype and excitement. London was doing its very best to emulate all that.

Annabel's (a private members club) in Berkeley Square (think Vera Lynn – 'A Nightingale Sang in Berkeley Square'), had the biggest and probably the most lavish Christmas frontage I have ever seen – a Christmas tree, four storeys high and created from sparkling gold lights with a huge, glittering silver star at the top, cascaded out in a triangle shape, down to street level, where a square, framed by ginormous candy canes, was formed to allow people to walk through the front door. Red and gold 'presents' in varying sizes had been strategically interspersed through the whole tree, to look like decorations. It was incredible to see and a real showstopper.

After a two-hour walk one Sunday with Mary and Symon, we'd ended up in Belgravia for lunch. Two cleverly motorised polar bears and their cubs were spending Christmas in the Paolo Moshino store window in Pimlico Road. Mama and papa bears' heads and arms and legs all moved, and the cubs constantly tumbled over each other. It was fabulous to watch, and Mary said she never tired of seeing it. Each year, people asked the staff when the polar bears would be returning from the North Pole. That's how popular it was.

New Zealand chef, Peter Gordon had a restaurant, Providores, in Marylebone High Street. Providores was making and selling cute gingerbread biscuits in the shape of a kiwi, with its long beak and face dipped in chocolate. I just had to get some of those, thinking they'd make a great token Christmas gift for London friends, old and new. So when I saw that Marylebone High Street was having its own Christmas Light Up, I decided to go.

Fairy lights were strung across the High Street from frontage to frontage, and enormous sparkling silver stars and evergreen Christmas tree frames had been fixed high up on lampposts, all the way down the street. The boutiques in the High Street were dazzling ordinarily, but made even more so, decorated and lit up in the early evening. Enormous swathes of *faux* tree branches and ivy framed some shop windows and doorways, with fairy lights entwined through it all. Others had huge red bows and gold bells over the doors, creating such a festive look and atmosphere.

The Rana Grocer shop was so Christmassy, staging bowls of oranges studded with cloves and twists of cinnamon sticks and a whole nutmeg tied into the pretty ribbon around them. The smell was heavenly. Diptique's window was aglow with huge candles and tea-light candles twinkling inside miniature two-storeyed, porcelain houses. An enormous glass snow globe, filled with a wooden nativity scene and fake snow falling, sat inside a giant-sized Mason mixing bowl. It looked fabulous. Each shop had embraced the theme and embodied the Christmas spirit in its own special way.

Most of the street was blocked off and shops and restaurants had stalls set up in the middle, offering a little of what they sold inside. There were many takers of the mulled wine being offered to leisurely shoppers. Heady aromas mingled in the air with Christmas carols and the shrieks of excited children, on a high at being out in the dark night and given treats from the stalls.

In my kitchen the next day I tried to replicate Peter Gordon's delectable gingerbread kiwis, spending an hour and a half making a huge mess and dripping chocolate all over the floor. Mine turned out a sad and lumpy version, with some looking like elephants, others like hippos and some even like polar bears.

Grinning like an idiot at my useless imitations, I uploaded a photo to Facebook of *my* gingerbread kiwis surrounding one of Peter Gordon's, with the caption: 'One of these things is not like the other, one of these things just doesn't belong', asking friends if they could possibly tell which was the odd one out. Talk about laugh. Everyone could *immediately* tell which was Peter Gordon's and which were the amateur/home-made/Annemarie versions. Ah well, it's the thought that counts … I knew my English friends would be *terribly* polite when receiving them, even if they were an abomination!

November Snippets

My book club girls – Anne, Monica, Laura and Jenni, were a delightful bunch of women. We'd meet monthly, taking turns to host and choosing a book we'd all read before the next get-together. Once hugs and kisses and shrieks of 'Hello, how are you!' were out the way and the drinks poured, we'd settle down.

The book would get a ten-minute look-in before the conversation went off into many divergent tangents, and several hours would pass in a blur of wine, chat and laughter. Each woman was interested, interesting, intelligent and great fun. We all became firm friends and I felt so lucky to have them in my life.

London does Christmas on a scale I've never seen the likes of. Not just the pubs, boutiques, big stores and businesses, but everyday homes are all lit up too. Sometimes after dinner we'd go out just to see the fairy lights wrapped around trees, some threaded through hedges, gates and pot plants, and candles glowing in the window. Christmas trees and tinsel twinkled at us through the open curtains. All this, being bundled up against the frosty cold, the anticipation and build-up, made Christmas so special and heart-warming. I loved it all.

The following link will take you directly to photos associated with November. Feel free to comment on any of them.

https://bit.ly/LLA_November-2018

DECEMBER 2018

THE ROMANOVS EXHIBITION; A HAMPER SURPRISE; CHRISTMAS IN CORNWALL

The cold was really setting in, and some days were quite miserable, with the rain and the damp almost seeping into our bones. Other days were just heavenly. The weather never deterred us though, from getting out and walking. Always there was something beautiful to see and admire, no matter the season, especially in the parks, with ghostly bare trees, frosty grass crunching underfoot and the air stilled and misty with suspended raindrops.

Night was falling early, and skies were now dark by 4.15 p.m. Our curtains were tightly drawn against the chill, the plump, goose-down winter duvet was on the bed and the radiators hummed, giving a comforting warmth to the flat. With the shorter, cooler days, came a less hurried life. No riverside cups of tea or glasses of wine for the foreseeable future and, looking out the window, through the now bare branches of the trees, our bench seat looked sad, damp and empty.

Bridget and Richard came down from Northants for an overnight stay at Anne's B&B and the four of us had a fabulous afternoon at the Russian Royalty, The Romanovs exhibition, on at the Queen's Gallery at Buckingham Palace. The detailed portraiture and the few items of Fabergé on display were just exquisite. One little treasure was the *Mosaic Egg with Surprise*. It was incredible. Made in 1914, the design was inspired by needlepoint, and it's regarded as one of the most technically accomplished and expensive Fabergé eggs ever made. The 'surprise' is an enamelled profile group portrait of the five children of Nicholas and Alexandra Feodorovna, made of platinum, enamel, diamonds, rubies, topaz, sapphires, garnets, moonstone and seed pearls. It was so delicate and fragile-looking and would have taken incredible skill to create.

Mid-December I had an entire day to myself, not needing to be anywhere or do anything. I booked an early slot to see the Gingerbread City exhibition at one of my favourite museums in the world, the V&A. I never tired of wandering through there and always used the front entrance, just so I could spend a few minutes to admire the magnificent and extravagant Chihuly chandelier – a masterpiece of twisted and turned, blown glass in blended shades of pale blues, lime greens and yellows. It is suspended from the V&A rotunda and hangs 27 feet long. Not only does it illuminate the foyer but it's also an incredible work of art.

The Gingerbread City exhibition was outstanding and was exactly what the title suggested – an edible city made totally of gingerbread, complete with a roller coaster, railway network, skyscrapers, highways and bridges, rooftop gardens, schools and homes. The coloured icings, chocolate touches and moulded jellies all added to the jaw-dropping and drooling experience. It was a visual feast, designed by seventy-one architectural companies. Everything was named – Sugar High Line, The Hanging Gardens of Honeycomb, Sweet Peaks, Bakewell Bridge, Tooth Fairy Terraces and so on. Each a work of art and so detailed.

This really was an exhibition for children, but I appreciated the work gone into creating this city. The lingering aroma was so mouth-watering and so tempting and it dawned on me, standing there looking, why there were so many staff in attendance – to stop little fingers from poking and swiping and licking all that deliciousness!

It was all too much and, with my tummy rumbling, I made my way down to the magnificent tea rooms on the ground floor – which are a visual feast themselves – to have a sticky bun and coffee. The tea rooms date back to the 1860s and were the first 'refreshment' rooms in any museum in the world. Again, it's a place I make a beeline for as it's so beautifully tiled, creating vistas of a time in history.

Sated, I hauled myself up and left the V&A, weaving my way at a gentle stroll through the SW1 area of London, taking in the stunning Forever Rose boutique which sells only roses, sending them all around the world. Lush and luxurious shop frontages and windows displays have always made me stop to gawp at what I couldn't afford. The softest cashmere pashminas in rich colours, cardigans and jerseys, handbags, shoes and outrageously expensive sunglasses (which looked like something Dame Edna Everage would wear), were elegantly draped or placed on mannequins, exquisitely poised to great effect.

In Grosvenor Square stands a life-sized brass sculpture of a lioness hunting a lesser kudu (antelope). It is superbly crafted and tactile, with muscles and skin so defined and taut. In these gardens I came across a live elf, who'd come all the way from Lithuania. With white bobbed hair, dressed in red boots, red leggings and a short, red fur-trimmed puffa coat, cinched in at her tiny waist by a wide black belt, this delightful young woman looked very much like an elf. Well, it was nearly Christmas, so I couldn't be making it up, could I?

In any climate, December is a busy month of planning, present and food shopping and cooking. It was ten days until Christmas Day, and we had one more drinks party to attend, then Murdoch and my niece, Victoria were coming for dinner on the 20th. That would be the last of the London festivities. We'd known for months that the two of them would each be going to their own Christmas Day events, known as the London Orphans Christmas. These are fun and companionable get-togethers on Christmas Day, for those living in London without parents or family in the UK. How they all managed to get to wherever it was, I don't know, as there is no public transport on Christmas Day in London.

We weren't going to stand in their way and, knowing they already had plans, I'd booked Christmas for us in Cornwall, staying four nights in St Ives and two nights in Penzance. Christmas lunch was booked at Tregenna Castle, for an eye-watering amount of money. However, I was so excited to be going to Cornwall as Penzance had been on my bucket list ever since I read Rosamunde Pilcher's book *The Shell Seekers*, and others set in such an historic and stunning part of England.

Late one afternoon in mid-December, we'd arrived home just before dusk. I'd put the kettle on for a cup of tea when our buzzer went, down at the main door.

"Afternoon, I have a large hamper for you. Is there anyone there who can help me bring it up the stairs, please?" said a voice through the intercom.

"You mean for Flat 12?" I asked, thinking he'd got the wrong place.

"Yes, are you Annemarie Rawson?"

"Yes, that's me. Thank you. Wait a moment and my husband will come down." Neither of us could fathom what it could possibly be. We weren't expecting any parcels.

Steve went down to help while nosy me hung over the banister, watching the two of them lumber up the three flights with this beautiful wicker basket between them. What on earth was this about?

Thanking the delivery man profusely and shutting the door

behind him, I knelt to undo the leather straps holding the lid in place. Oh, my goodness! What a treasure chest of foodie heaven. On the top was a whole side of hot-smoked salmon, potted Stilton, two French cheeses and a Wiltshire cured ham, all resting on a flat bag of ice. Nestled further into the straw were chutneys, cheese biscuits, jars of Christmas mince, olives, a Christmas pudding, two bottles of bubbles, two bottles of chianti and a chablis. Shortbread, chocolates, and crackers were hidden more deeply.

"Bloody hell," whispered Steve. I looked up at him, just as incredulous, seeing the amount of food and what it must have cost. I couldn't believe my eyes. Who could possibly have sent this? To us?

I checked the label on the lid and yes, it *was* meant for us. Taped under the label was an envelope. The mystery was about to be solved. Inside was a beautiful thank-you card:

'Annemarie & Steve, thank you so much for everything you did to get the flat ready for sale and then sold. A fantastic result. I couldn't have done it without you. Merry Christmas. Caroline.'

I was so shocked but simultaneously thrilled to bits. How incredibly generous of Caroline to do this. She'd paid me already but was so delighted to get it sold she sent this foodie-heaven hamper. It was gratefully received, with relish – if you'll pardon the pun!

Lucky Murdoch and Victoria would get to enjoy the spoils too when they came for dinner. Already I'd planned an entrée of smoked salmon and roasted beetroot with a horseradish dressing. Does that tickle the taste buds? It certainly tickled mine.

The skies may have been steely grey, with ponderous clouds scudding above us, but St Ives did not disappoint, one bit. After four train journeys (all easily done, just crossing a platform for each leg) we arrived at St Ives station.

"Smell that!" said Steve, dropping our bags on the platform, then stepping off the train, taking in the expansive view of the bay. The sandy beach had a few hardy souls on it, well rugged up against the chill, hands pushed deeply into pockets and heads bent against the breeze. Gulls were cawing, catching the updraughts, and drifting wherever the wind took them.

The salty tang of the sea air certainly filled our lungs as we pulled our bags along behind us and followed the path from the station car park, leading down into the bustling centre. The town, with its fishermen's cottages and pretty shops, cobbled, narrow and steep streets, was instantly captivating. Flower baskets hung everywhere, doing their best to thrive in the cool weather, and the cute shop frontages filled with light, food and gifts were tantalising. My thighs and calves protested loudly climbing the hill to our little Airbnb, being too used to the flat streets of London.

Tapping in the code, we pushed open our sea-blue front door and immediately stepped into the kitchen area. The wide, white-painted floorboards, white-timbered walls and tiny mosaic tiles decorating the bathroom made it such a sweet and charming cottage. Lovely seaside and nautical touches added to the coastal ambiance. The owners had made it so homely and welcoming, and with quality soft furnishings too. It was tiny but perfect for two. Us two! Quickly we unpacked. I couldn't wait to get back down into the town.

Steep steps cut into a side street led us down to the main street where colourful bunting, strung up from side to side and all the way through, flapped in the light breeze. Finding ourselves on the waterfront, I could hear live music coming from one of the bars. "Let's stop here, Steve." I nodded into the bar. "The music's good but it looks pretty chocka inside. What do you think?"

"We could sit out here if you think you'll be warm enough." He indicated the long table, tucked under the veranda and out of the way of the breeze.

"I'll be fine. Look, they provide blankets. I'll throw one over my legs. Hang on, I'll check with these guys if they'd mind sharing."

Two men in their forties sat at one end of the table with their cute sausage dogs, one on each lap. "All good. They're very happy to share. I'll have a red wine please." Steve went in while I plonked myself down, stroking the silky ears of the dog closest to me. The three of us got chatting. Yes, *I know*! It just happens; don't ask me how. These two guys were down from Shrewsbury with their 'girls' – the two cute dogs, who had on their Christmas jerseys to keep the chill off them. Well, they *were* very low to the ground.

These two gents were having Christmas together in a rented cottage, not wanting to book a restaurant. They'd crammed their car full of special treats and food, as well as a dozen bottles of wine, so they were well and truly set for a big Christmas Day. Steve arrived back with the drinks, and we passed a very convivial hour and a half with them – sorting out Brexit and the rest of the nation's problems.

Pulling on our winter woollies the next morning we took the steps down again to the town and had a brisk walk around the beach front. Eight hardy surfers sat out on their boards, bobbing on the swell, waiting to catch a wave. I shivered, thinking how cold they must be, but they were in full neoprene wetsuits with hoods. A couple of crazy people had stripped down to their undies and run into the water. Madness. Surprisingly, the air temperature wasn't cold at all at around 10–11 °C but I can't bear to be cold, so with all my layers on, was just right.

An older gentleman fell into step with us on the blustery Southwest Coast Path and accompanied us most of the way, pointing out local bits of interest. "Is this your first time in St Ives?" he asked, mid-stride.

"Yes, it is. I've wanted to come here for years, though," I told him, pushing my wind-blown hair back off my face. "You?"

"Oh no!" he chuckled. "I come every year for Christmas. I just love it here. I even let the missus come along." He looked sideways at me, grinning, never missing a step.

"Heavens! Why do you come at this time of year? It's cold and blustery. Don't you want to come and have the sun on your back in summer?"

"Good grief! No thank you. Not with the hordes of tourists, swarming through the streets at that time. It's so much better now. Look at this place." He swung one arm wide, encapsulating the view across the hill, out to sea and the beach below, dotted with only a few dog walkers and the intrepid surfers.

"I know, you're right. It is lovely," I replied, looking out at it all. "I'd hate the push and shove of the summer trade too."

"Right, well I'll have to leave you here at the chapel. I'm taking this other path now. I hope you have a splendid Christmas while here. If you're looking for coffee after this, the only place open will be the Sloop Inn. Down there at the waterfront." He pointed and added, "Very nice to have met you and chatted."

We said our goodbyes and thanked him for his company and, with a hand raised in farewell, he was off. We turned to read the plaque fixed to the ancient stone wall of St Nicholas Chapel, sitting right at the top of the island. It had been there since the fourteenth century and is simply but beautifully built. In the eighteenth century, smugglers were known to be using the beaches below to land their illicit goods, so the revenue officers would watch from the chapel for any activity. Funnily enough, sometimes the smugglers would use it to keep a watch for the revenue officers. I wonder if they ever banged into each other!

Sure enough, the only place open for coffee was The Sloop Inn, an eighteenth-century pub. It's described as a classic old fishermen's pub, complete with low ceilings, tankards behind the bar and a comprehensive selection of Cornish ales. It's a favourite haunt of locals, anglers, artists and tourists all year round, with only a cobbled forecourt and road separating it from the sea. Steve and I slipped into a booth, looking forward to our coffee.

The pub was starting to fill up when we left and, in hindsight, we should have stayed there for lunch. At £85 each for Christmas lunch (wine extra) at Tregenna Castle my expectations and anticipation were up there for a beautiful three-course dinner. The castle and grounds were stunning, but inside I'd politely label it as 'faded glory'. What must have been the ballroom had become the Christmas Day dining room and was as cold as charity – in terms of ambiance.

Sadly, lunch was very disappointing and after pushing my grey Brussels sprouts around the plate, once I found them swimming in the lake of gravy, I moved it to one side. Steve ate because he was hungry but was horribly disappointed as well. As soon as he was done, we left, grumbling our way down the path and back to our cottage. It didn't pay to think of our usual Christmas Day fare, albeit outdoors in a New Zealand summer. I knew they were feeding a crowd at the Castle, but the Brussels sprouts looked and tasted as though they'd been boiled — since 8.00 a.m. Our evening was spent back in the Sloop Inn, having a much better time, enjoying a couple of drinks and good company.

After breakfast the following day, we hiked up to the crest of the road before taking the steps at Porthmeor Hill and down beside the Tate St Ives. Lots of people were on the beach walking dogs, and more surfers were in the sea. The town was so busy, with more cafés and bars open and the waterfront was jam-packed, with everyone out loving the tepid sun after the grey gloom of the last three days. We managed to grab a spot on the upper deck of a café and enjoyed people-watching from our little vantage spot before wandering through the cobbled streets ourselves. Art galleries were bursting with paintings of the seaside and fishermen's cottages, and cute boutiques sold all sorts of nautical décor and local crafts. Being Boxing Day, we knew the Barbara Hepworth Museum and Sculpture Garden would be closed. That would have to wait for another trip.

I'd been hoping to bump into the 'boys' and the 'girls' we'd spent an enjoyable time with on our first evening in St Ives, as the older one had whispered to me he was going to propose to the younger one on Christmas Day. I was dying to find out if he'd said yes.

Leaving St Ives on the train, we rumbled through to Penzance, an ancient market town and popular tourist spot, to stay in a 300-year-old inn, just across the road from the railway and bus stations. Penzance is only 10 miles from Land's End and is surrounded by nature's beauty and full of Celtic culture and history.

We checked in quickly, dropped our bags, grabbed a takeaway coffee and jumped on the next bus that would take us to the Minack Theatre. It's an open-air theatre, much like a Roman amphitheatre and is set into the cliff face of Porthcurno, with a rocky granite outcrop jutting into the sea.

Our double-decker bus trundled its way through narrow hedgerows and tight hairpin bends, working its way down, down, down slippery roads, through dank woods with overhead branches scraping the paint off the upper deck, and stopping at obscure places to drop off or collect people. It then climbed again to reach beautiful sunshine and magnificent views of field after field of daffodils and lush patchwork pastures, intersected with hedges forming the seams of the 'quilt'. Varfell Farms, just outside Penzance, grow 500 million daffodils from December to early April, which are handpicked and mostly exported. Such a mind-boggling number.

On we went, past a circle of stones, purported to be a group of young girls (The Merry Maidens of Boleigh) who were dancing at a pagan ritual, and minstrels (Stone Pipers) who played for them. These stones are reckoned to be 5,000 years old and the maidens looked like a miniature of Stonehenge.

It had turned into the most glorious day, with clear blue skies, warm sunshine and no wind. Porthcurno Beach and its clifftops were breathtaking, and the Minack Theatre more so. This masterpiece creation was the brainchild of Miss Rowena Cade, who lived in Minack House above the theatre. She was a strong and formidable woman, having done a lot of the carving out herself with hand tools and carrying sand up from the beach. Managing to hew seating and statues out of the cliff face would have been back-breaking work. Plays and concerts are performed during the summer months, and shuttle buses run from all points around Cornwall so people can come to enjoy this delightful place.

I couldn't visit Cornwall without sampling a Cornish pasty. Inside the Minack café, we snaffled a fabulous seat by the window, looking out over the clifftops, the beach and the sea rolling in. Our pasty was divine – tender, full of flavoursome steak and potato chunks wrapped in a dense but light pastry.

Cornwall has a great history of smugglers and hidden treasure and I've always loved watching the TV series *Poldark*. The leading man, who plays the title character, has been chosen for his smouldering good looks, luscious curly black hair, and impossibly fit body.

Our waitress had been so friendly and greeted us with, "'Ello my lovelies, 'ow can I 'elp you today," so I couldn't help but ask, "What time will Poldark be riding across the cliff top? I'd really love to get a photo."

Well, she called my bluff beautifully and said, "Funny you should ask that, m'dear. You've just missed him and sadly, he won't be back today. He and Demelza often walk hand-in-hand along the beach below. And ..." she drew in a long breath and her eyes glazed over, "sometimes he strips off his shirt, gets down to his breeches and goes in for a swim. We have excellent binoculars up here, you know." She gave me a nod and a wink.

At that we both burst out laughing. Poldark is filmed all over Cornwall, and Porthcurno happens to be one of the places they come to. I wondered if I could get a job in that café, always keeping those binoculars close to hand ...

Aside from Poldark, Porthcurno is where the first transatlantic cable came into England, from Portugal, and was laid in 1870. It has a fascinating history and during the First and Second World Wars, the area was filled with soldiers protecting the cables from sabotage.

On the return journey our bus driver kindly dropped us off at a random spot so we could walk down through a village called Paul to the pretty fishing village of Mousehole (pronounced 'Mousill' – Cornish speak, I'm guessing). It was very busy with winter holidaymakers, just like us and Steve and I popped in and out the few little shops around the waterfront. The blustery, seafront promenade walk returned us an hour later to Penzance for dinner in our pub.

St Michael's Mount, Cornwall's reflection of the French *Mont St Michel*, was exceptional. I loved its beauty, both inside and out. An ancient castle, it is still home to the St Aubyn family who've lived there for over 200 years. I sometimes struggled with the history of these places, coming from such a young country as New Zealand.

At Marazion, a ten-minute drive from Penzance, a large group of us waited for the 1.35 p.m. low tide to walk across the causeway to St Michael's. Some people just couldn't wait and had removed socks and shoes, rolled up trousers and started wading. In winter? Madness. There's a little boat trip available to ferry you over at a minimal cost, but I wanted to walk the causeway – keeping my feet dry.

We'd spent a lovely morning exploring Penzance, taking a taxi down to Marazion, opting to walk back after our tour of St Michael's. We stopped to eat Cornish ice cream, loving the views from the sea wall on our meander back to our inn.

What a brilliant break away from London. There's so much of Cornwall to see and explore and we only saw a little corner of it. We loved our time, and everyone was so warm, friendly and welcoming, with lots of 'my lovely, my love, darlin'. Just a shame I never got to see Poldark on horseback, galloping across the clifftops ...

Do go to St Ives and Penzance for a Christmas break – just thoroughly check out where you're going to have Christmas lunch!

It was back to London then for a rollicking New Year's Eve party at Anne and Richard's. It was going to be a doozy and I was so looking forward to it.

December Snippets

La Salon Privé. While Bridget and Richard were with us we had a superb lunch at an elegant little French restaurant called La Salon Privé in St Margaret's – between Twickenham and Richmond. It's the loveliest little area. I don't remember what we ate but do remember that it was all delicious, classically French with a contemporary twist and good portions – all from the Menu du Jour. Le Salon Privé is beautifully done inside and out, with fabulously coloured and patterned lead-light windows and entrance canopy.

Zoran's. Apart from the French restaurant, we'd also fallen in love with a very European café called Zoran's Delicatessen, across the road from Le Salon Privé. Offering a selection of European provisions (pastas, sauces, panettone, tinned beans, olives, peppers) and beautifully prepared and presented fresh salads, lasagne, cakes and muffins, it was futile to resist at times. Steve and I often shared a coconut and raspberry muffin with our coffee and a great chat with Zoran when he was there. He was such a likeable, friendly man. Sitting in the café I could pretend I was somewhere in Continental Europe.

The tables were tightly fitted in, some with small bench seating along one wall and others with bentwood chairs tucked in. There were always tantalising cooking aromas wafting up the short flight of stairs from the kitchen – chorizo sizzling in the pan was the best. We often headed for Zoran's while out walking or shopping in Twickenham. It has become an institution in St Margaret's café society.

The following link will take you directly to photos associated with December. Feel free to comment on any of them.

https://bit.ly/LLA_December-2018

JANUARY 2019
SIR JOHN SOANE MUSEUM; RHS WISLEY

Sadly, our New Year's Eve party never eventuated. Poor Richard came down with nasty flu and was confined to bed. Awful for him and a shame for the rest of us but couldn't be helped. Knowing this, I rushed off to the supermarket and Steve and I sat down that night to a special dinner of pork wellington (my version of beef wellington), steamed Brussels sprouts, green beans and toasted carrots. I quickly tossed the cooked carrots in a hot pan with a little olive oil, a teaspoon of honey and cumin seeds in a hot pan, before serving. Dessert was stewed apples and figs (frozen during summer), cooked with a little ground ginger, cinnamon and mixed spice, adding Greek yoghurt to it, to serve. It was all so good, washed down with a shared bottle of wine and followed by Roquefort and crackers.

With dishes cleared, we perched ourselves on the back of the sofa, a glass of port in hand, and saw in the New Year, accompanied by the bang and whizz of fireworks going off all over Teddington.

January skies were heavy and grey, everywhere was damp underfoot and moisture was thick in the air. A watery sun endeavoured to push through but was only ever fleeting.

January is purported to be slow and quiet, with people back at work and recovering physically and financially from Christmas, as well as hunkering down and keeping warm at home.

While family and friends in New Zealand and Australia were sweltering in temperatures of 29–30 and 42 °C respectively, we ventured out, fully kitted up in our woollies when it was 3 °C in London. This day out was to an area new to us – Broadway Market, out by Bethnal Green and near London Fields, to enjoy hot and jellied eel for lunch. Don't be ridiculous! I couldn't think of anything worse. Oh yes, I could. Oysters. They were on sale too – slimy, cream and grey-looking, floating in a stinky brine. I was almost retching. But jellied eel *was* a staple for locals, back in the day. We settled instead for hot-off-the-plate Turkish breads stuffed with spinach and cheese or potato, onion and chilli, which we watched being prepared in the café window. What a fantastic way to show off their food and lure people in. The queue was out the door, and I was salivating, awaiting our turn.

Back on the tube, we jumped off at Holborn to visit the Sir John Soane Museum. This is a must-see as Sir John was a collector of the extraordinary and one of London's eminent neo-classicist architects. He was the son of a bricklayer but made his fortune through his architecture. He designed the Dulwich Picture Gallery, which had become a favourite of ours.

The museum (three homes that he purchased from the late eighteenth century onwards) has been left much as it was 180 years ago. Sir John demolished and rebuilt the three houses, connecting each and incorporating all his architectural styles. It was fabulous and his collection of Egyptian and Roman antiquities was incredible – including a 3,000-year-old sarcophagus, which had been rejected by the British Museum. He bought it (in the nineteenth century) for £2,000. It was bizarre he'd purchased all these things, but never left the UK.

"Have you been out to Wisley yet, Annemarie?" A text message had popped up from Anne (B&B).

"No. It's on the list. It looks gorgeous and comes highly recommended."

"Well how about we go next Friday? I'll drive us. We could leave at about 9.30 a.m. and have coffee when we arrive. I'm a member but sadly, I can only take a family member as a guest. You okay to pay?" she asked.

"Of course I am! How lovely. And yes, Friday is good for me. I'll walk around to yours. Thanks, Anne. See you then."

It was a grey day when Anne drove us to RHS Wisley in Surrey for lunch and to enjoy the Winter Walk. Wisley would become a favourite place as it's beautiful all year round. The gardens seem to go on forever, packed with inspiration for every sort of gardener. The Great Brick Safari was also on in the glasshouse, which is like stepping into a jungle, being home to exotic and tropical plants. Animals and plants made from Lego were hidden amongst the foliage and squeals of delight as children chanced upon them, could be heard all over the glasshouse. It was great fun. And, as with Kew, the gift shop was compelling, full of botanical books and prints, cards and tea towels and table napkins, with the fabulous Emma Bridgewater crockery available too. Anne and I both bought a 'seconds' mug which depicts plants and the old buildings of Wisley. I love it and always use it at home.

The sun decided to come out for our last hour of wandering, making everything look even better. We'd pack a picnic and come back in the summertime. After a great pub lunch at The Anchor, sitting on the very pretty Pyrford Lock, Anne drove me over the single-lane little bridge to show me the church built in 1140 where she and Richard were married. It was so tiny inside, they only just managed to fit their guests in for the wedding ceremony.

January Snippet

Appreciating my life. Mid-January, I finished a refurbishing interiors job I'd started in October. It was fun hunting out fabrics, buying cushions and throws for the sitting room, organising tradesmen and ordering new blinds for the kitchen. One daughter's bedroom had also been de-cluttered, storing her remaining treasures in bins under the bed. Excess furniture was collected up and taken to a lock-up unit. Everything had come together well and looked so good. I had a happy client. Well, happy with the job I'd done.

What I discovered during my working days, was just how stressed so many people were. One client was running a company and constantly had to win contracts. She never stopped worrying as there was a hefty mortgage and staff to be paid. Her life was torn between family, home and work and there were many sleepless nights and migraine headaches.

One cleaning client had a young family and a nanny who came in at 7.00 a.m. and left at 5.30 p.m., or when the mother or father returned home. Mum did four days at the office and one day at home. One morning while I was there, she was tapping away at her laptop while the youngest was sleeping and the other two were at school. I put a cup of coffee down beside her. She burst into tears and the stress poured out. The gist of it was that she hated her job, hated having to leave her children, but had a huge mortgage and annual holidays to Europe to pay for. The poor woman felt that she was a bad mother and a bad employee because she couldn't give 100 per cent to either. It wasn't my place to give advice; I just listened, murmured the appropriate noises and rubbed her shoulder. It was so sad.

As to two other employers, one was so stressed that she

frequently vomited, and the other was a whirling dervish, achieving very little, while constantly saying how much she had to get done.

All of them were like mice on a wheel, unable to get off and it didn't take me very long to realise just how fortunate I was.

The following link will take you directly to photos associated with January. Feel free to comment on any of them.

https://bit.ly/LLA_January-2019

FEBRUARY 2019
MALTA; HIGHGATE CEMETERY AND SURROUNDINGS; HAMPSTEAD HEATH AND PONDS

Woo hoo! Malta here we come. We both looked forward to being a little warmer there than London.

Malta Passport Control was a breeze, as ours was the only flight in, and after a twenty-minute bus ride we arrived in Valletta – the capital, draped in a cold, wet drizzle. So much for the warmer weather. Home for the next five nights was perfectly situated in a little street between the main one, Republic, and the other full of cafés and restaurants, called Merchant. After a quick recce of the apartment and leaving the unpacking until later, we walked the wall around the city. Let me just say, Valletta is stunning. The limestone is beautiful – even the crumbly bits – and so striking in the sunshine, when it finally made an appearance. The reflection of the light on the limestone was intense, sometimes making it hard to look up without sunglasses on.

Malta was the headquarters of the Knights of St John, and it was they who ordered the building of the St John's Co-Cathedral. It's called a co-cathedral because there came a time historically when it achieved equal prominence to the older Cathedral of St Paul in Mdina, so now both buildings are considered 'sees' (or seats) of the Bishop of Malta. Austere on the outside, it was originally the same on the inside, but is now so ornate that it was hard to know where to look and what to focus on. The entire floor is covered with marble tombstones, commemorating some of the most illustrious knights of the Order. Some of whom came from powerful European aristocratic families.

Malta is such an historic place. We loved it and soaked it all up. It's been invaded so many times, hence the massive fortifications and huge walls, and ruled by so many nations. The British entered the fray when the French took over and started looting the Maltese churches to fund Bonaparte's charge into Egypt. The Maltese revolted against the French and asked Britain for assistance. Collectively, they ousted the French and Malta became a British colony, gaining independence in September 1964. In May 2004 Malta went on to become part of the EU.

We meandered back through the old narrow streets, watching men shimmying up ladders, erecting banners which criss-crossed so many streets. Nosy me asked what it was all about. It was St Paul's Feast Day that Sunday, 10 February. It's known as St Paul's Shipwreck Day and the story tells us that the Apostle Paul was being taken to Rome to be tried as a political rebel, but the ship carrying him and some 274 others was caught in a violent storm, only to be wrecked two weeks later on the Maltese coast. All of them survived, managing to swim ashore. Malta celebrates with music, dance and all-day church services but most importantly, never-ending parades from Friday night through to Sunday night. It would be quite a spectacle and Steve and I once again were lucky, having stumbled upon festivities in most places we went.

The Hop On/Hop Off bus took us on the tour north to the beautiful town of Mdina. The sun was out but it was still far too cold for me to continue sitting on the open top, so I left Steve to it, opting for the warmth of the bus interior. The tour took in other towns and seaside resorts, but the larger spots were St Julian and Sliema, before returning to Valletta.

In the town of Rabat, we climbed stairs to have coffee in an elevated café with the most glorious view of the countryside. Our table was bumped by a very elegant, older woman squeezing through the narrow gap. I edged our table over a little to aid her passage when she snorted, "I'm not that fat, you know!"

I grinned at her, and she grinned at me while I blustered, "Of course you're not. I was just trying to make it a little easier".

Well, that's all it took. She and her husband sat at the empty table beside us, entertaining us while we drank coffee and shared a slice of almond and orange cake. She, Mary, had been born in a little house in Mdina, 80 years ago. She left the island when she was 30 and she and her husband, who was English, lived and ran restaurants in Manchester, returning to Malta when they retired. So she was back to her roots and loved their simple life.

After all that exploring, we were late having lunch. It was 3.00 p.m. and we were both ravenous. I'd seen delicious salads being served in Merchant Street the day before, so we grabbed a table and managed to score the last of them. The salad was a rainbow of colours and just superb. It was especially good after a disastrous dinner the previous night in a restaurant that had been recommended by the couple who owned our accommodation. The traditional dish in Malta is rabbit stew and we were both keen to try it – done in lots of red wine and rosemary. What arrived on our plates was a mess of bones with stringy meat attached. Good flavour, yes, but it was certainly not a hearty stew. Accompanying our 'bones' was the smallest ramekin of soggy roasted potatoes and another of watery cabbage and overdone courgettes. It all looked so limp and unappetising and was very disappointing. The saving grace of the evening was a fabulous bottle of red to help ease our 'digestion'.

Lunch done and dusted we clambered up the street to see the other side of Valletta, from the Upper Barraka gardens, with a view over the Saluting Battery. I was stopped by an older English lady.

"Excuse me dear, are you a local?" she asked, tapping me on the arm.

"No, sorry, I'm not. Are you all right? Do you need something?" I checked with her.

"No, no. I just thought you might be local and might know where the cannons were and when they might be fired. I'm blowed if we can find them," she said indicating her friend.

"Well, we're on our way, if you want to follow us. It's just up here."

"Ooh, thank you, dear. Come along, Judith," she said, taking her friend by the arm. "Now, my name's Muriel. Me and my friend Judith are from Newcastle and ..." *And* she didn't draw breath until we arrived at the Battery. Steve, keeping step on the other side of me, gave me a discreet nudge, grinning and whispering, "You've met your match there!" But she was no match; she beat me hands down in the talking stakes.

Muriel and Judith babbled on during the firing and it was while we were watching one of the guards below, swilling water onto the two guns that had been fired, that dear Muriel from Newcastle piped up, "What on earth is he doing that for when there's a battery in there?"

I had to look away while I grinned inanely. Muriel had no idea that a battery is what a collection of cannons is called – typically six in a row (I did look that number up, to be honest). It was so funny.

The streets that night became a cacophony of blasting whistles, singing, trumpets and drums and people. Everyone was jostling for prime position in the procession, which we followed to the church to drop off an extremely heavy effigy of St Paul, who'd been triumphantly hoisted and balanced on the shoulders of eight strapping men and paraded through the streets. It was the start of the celebration of his feast day, the only winter feast day in Malta.

The brass bands were out in force in a fierce competition to outdo each other. All of Malta was on the street. The church was the last stop on the way to our apartment and, as soon as we'd finished dinner, we went back out on the streets to immerse ourselves in the palpable joy of the people. It was intoxicating.

There's no lie-in in Valletta on a Saturday morning. The church bells still ring furiously at 7.30 a.m. on the weekend. It was such a glorious morning and I just wanted to wander a little, then stop for coffee before we hit the tourist spots. It was just on 10.00 a.m. when I saw people slipping behind a heavy, burgundy-coloured curtain, hung in a doorway, so we did too. From a very ordinary exterior we stepped into this stunning, light-filled church. Mass was just starting so we tiptoed along the back where an elderly priest was either deep in prayer or having a little snooze ... On every trip and almost every church I enter, I light a candle – and have a little chat in my head with whoever might listen, to help someone who's sick or to make life better for someone else. I took a moment before silently tiptoeing out, squinting into the bright sunshine.

Up another side street we stopped for coffee where the tables were bathed in sunshine. Coffee arrived at the table next to us in a sort of decanter with two glasses on the side. It was really unusual and neither of us had seen that before. We just opted for the usual cappuccino and a double shot Americano.

The Knights Hospitallers was a military order and the museum known as The Knights Hospitallers Museum was the first visit on the day's agenda. Originally an underground hospital for all, set up by the Knights of St John, it was a fascinating stop where we could travel through 700 years of history of the Knights of St John including the sights, smells and sounds. Next on the list and just across the road, was the St Elmo Fort and War Museum. The Fort played a major role during the 1565 Siege of Malta and was the scene of intense fighting during that siege. It withstood a bombardment from a Turkish cannon but fell to the Turks some 28 days after the attack. It was a fascinating place to visit. Obviously a strategic point during all Malta's war history, it had the most outstanding views.

Coffee-to-go in hand, we jumped on board a local bus going to the Blue Grotto. Most of the passengers emptied out for this special place, which is a complex of caves around the coast. The water is deep and beautifully clean and clear. When it's sunny, the light reflects off the sandy sea floor, lighting up the caves. We took the path leading down to the water to the boat tour which goes around the coastline and into the mouth of the caves, formed in the cliff faces. After hiking all the way down, we decided not to do the boat tour but walked back up to wait at the top for the return bus, along with a young French couple. What brilliant luck when a taxi pulled up, as the bus wasn't due back for another hour. The four of us shared the cost of the return to Valletta, making it a very economical journey.

Our taxi driver was shouting at us so loudly all the way back, in an attempt to make us understand what he was saying in English. I think a few of us have done that when travelling but shouting makes very little difference! It was funny but we were all very polite.

After another excellent salad lunch, we spent a glorious afternoon in the winter sunshine, strolling through the streets. With two bottles of wine under our arm and a little something for our dinner, we made our way down Main Street heading for home, listening to and watching the hub-bub of those who sat at the outdoor cafés, whiling away the afternoon with friends or family. It had been another memorable day in a beautiful, old and wonderfully historic place.

Our morning the next day started at 8.35 a.m., sitting on a full bus heading for the Marsaxlokk markets, Fishing Village and Floriana. Together on the bus we were a mixture of French, African, Japanese, Chinese, locals and of course, we two Kiwis. Steve and I had our ears pricked listening to the French women talk. They spoke slowly enough for me to understand some of what they were saying and, for Steve, a lot of what they were saying.

I nudged him and moved in closer. "I missed that bit," I whispered. Steve's shoulders were bouncing up and down with laughter he was trying desperately to hold in. "What did she say about her boyfriend?"

Finally pulling himself together, Steve whispered back, "I think she said he's a terrible kisser and has bad breath but doesn't know how to tell him!" We had a quiet giggle, not wanting the girls to realise Steve had understood their conversation. That was going to be a tricky conversation for her to have.

At the entrance to the market, the bus doors flew open and the contents (us), were disgorged into the middle of the road with the driver gesticulating madly, warning us of the cars passing him and to be careful.

Marsaxlokk is very rustic and charming, and sun umbrellas were up outside the cafés and restaurants, with some locals already sitting and sipping coffees from tiny cups, watching us tourists roll in. The little harbour shimmered and sparkled in the dazzling morning sun while brightly coloured boats bobbed up and down, everything combining to create a timeless, picturesque vista that probably hasn't changed for a century.

The market itself was typical of any European country town market – racks of clothing, stalls of make-up, leather (and fake) bags and belts, shoes and household items. The main attractions for me were the fresh food and fish stalls. The locals were busy stashing vegetables and fish into trundlers and cardboard boxes, all to be carried home and prepared for the long Sunday lunch with family.

There was minimal smell at the fish stalls, indicative of a fresh haul from the sea. Skilled fisherwomen, knives flashing as quick as lightning, sliced and diced, while craggy-faced, sea-hardy fishermen sat on barrels beside the water, squinting into the sun, their battered caps pulled low, while drinking a well-earned coffee and puffed on a cigarette.

Our coffee came out of the back of a van, courtesy of a Londoner from Wimbledon with such an entertaining patter that we stood and chatted with him while we drank his nutty-flavoured brew. Dave (our barista) was a true 'wheeler-dealer' who'd travelled the world, in between landscaping some of London's finest homes. He'd been living in Malta for six years with his Maltese wife and the only thing he missed about London was the green spaces. A lovely guy.

Steve and I jumped off the bus one stop early on the return journey as we'd spied a beautiful building on several of our trips in and out of Valletta and wanted to investigate. And yes, it was another church. Once again, Mass was in progress, so I discreetly lit another candle, had a brief chat with my deity and slipped quietly out the door.

This church is called St Publius and what was so special about it was the clock face on the right-hand tower. It says 28 April 1942, 7.50 a.m. This was Malta's darkest day when 63 aircraft dropped bombs all over Malta. St Publius' congregation had arrived for an 8.00 a.m. Mass and when the air raid siren went, they and the priest rushed to shelter in the crypt. The church took a direct hit, demolishing one of the towers and completely burying the people inside. When rescuers arrived and cleared the rubble away, 13 corpses were removed but the rest were alive, with varying injuries. The clock was deliberately set at that time to remember that awful day in Malta's history.

Being Sunday, at every church we passed Mass was in progress, or people were spilling out of the doors at the end of the service, congregating in the street in their finery for the obligatory exchange of family news before everyone dispersed to attend or cook the Sunday family lunch.

Valletta was bursting at the seams. So many people were beautifully turned out. Some women pushing prams wore stiletto, knee-high boots, dads looked just as well coiffed as the mums and little girls and boys emulated mama and papa's dress. The girls had their hair piled high on their heads, fake fur jerkins, cute boots and a wee cross-body bag. Many of the boys wore navy padded jackets, taupe trousers and navy sports shoes. Everyone was very glamorous, even grandmama and grandpapa.

Every outdoor café was full of the cheerful ambiance of relaxation and bonhomie. Bands played all over Valletta, and it was exactly like a ticker-tape parade to honour St Paul. We could hardly move in Merchant Street with the throng of people. Children made piles of the confetti, having great fun throwing it at each other. I nearly stood on one little boy who'd been buried in it. It was a fabulous spectacle, and we couldn't help but get caught up in it all. I asked a policeman if this was just all about St Paul and he said, "Yes, don't you do this at home?" Imagine the chaos in London. But not there.

The site of the Rampila restaurant was once a military lookout point, set in the mighty stronghold wall surrounding Malta and built by the Knights of St John, back in the sixteenth century. It was a special lunch for us, seated out on the terrace, with an historic view overlooking the magnificent entrance to Valletta. It was an early and wonderful birthday celebration for me. The service was excellent, and lunch arrived on the arm of a bow-tied, white-napkin-over-the-arm waiter, delivered with good humour and finesse.

The island of Gozo, seen through the window of the Hop On/Hop Off bus, was lush and green. Gozo 'feeds' everyone in the country and is so different from Malta. We'd caught a ferry across, which was frequent and inexpensive at €4.65 return for a journey of less than thirty minutes. Our travel around Malta was on local buses and, no matter how far we went, it cost €1.50 for two hours, jumping on and off wherever we liked.

Staying in the heart of the old town of Valletta was the best advice we received. It was easy to dash back to drop off shopping or have a reprieve at our little apartment. Do go to Malta to experience and learn of its extraordinary history and beauty and, if you can, time your visit to coincide with a feast day – you'll love the hype and the buzz of it all.

Our flight back to London was incredible, the path taking us over snow-covered Corsica, Nice and the Italian Alps. With my face and phone camera pressed to the window, the scenery was so close and defined; I could see the Italian viaduct motorways intersecting all the mountains and disappearing into miles of tunnels. Extraordinary to see.

We woke to a London 'pea-souper' but the forecast had the sun bursting through at 11.00 a.m. and that's exactly what happened. No time for Steve's usual Saturday morning sleep-in. Vogel sandwiches, *pain aux raisins*, sunblock and our coffee cups tightly wedged into my backpack, we were out the door at 9.45 a.m., looking forward to another great day out.

Highgate Cemetery had been in the news a couple of days earlier, as Karl Marx's London memorial had been vandalised for the second time with the words 'doctrine of hate' and 'architect of genocide' daubed in red paint. Awful. His grave is known to be one of the most visited in London. There are many high-profile and famous people buried in this cemetery but the most recent was George Michael who was interred in 2016, with his mother, for the princely sum of £18,325. Highgate tops the London list of cemeteries as being the most expensive place to be buried. The first burial there took place in 1839.

"Shall I book a plot for you, Steve? We might be able to tuck you in next to George," I teased, as we wandered.

He snorted. "Don't bother! I'll be a bag of dust and you can just scatter my ashes on a decent golf course somewhere. That'll do." He grinned at me and I shuddered. Such grisly thoughts on a beautiful day.

"C'mon," I took his hand, turned my face to the sun and moved him forward, to dispel unnecessary thoughts of death.

Tours run throughout the cemetery, which is split by a road and described as having east and west burial plots. An entrance fee is charged, which I'd never heard of to enter a cemetery, but I guess it covers the tours. Highgate doubles as a nature reserve too and is beautifully laid out and kept well. We strolled through, admiring the garden and pausing to read some of the historic headstones.

In the Highgate/Camden area wonderful architecture abounds and beautiful old houses were once bedsits for 'single women coming to London to be secretaries and nurses'. Now they are rather elegant, expensive flats. One street of these beauties was orchards before they were replaced by housing. Prior to that, the land and original villa were owned by Angela Burdett, the granddaughter of Thomas Coutts, founder of the bank Coutts & Co. They'd owned plenty in the area in their time.

On to Hampstead Heath – a wild area of woodland and meadows, sprawling over 800 acres with spectacular London views. The sunny weather brought out every man and his dog and people peeled off jackets and jerseys to absorb the warmth of an early spring sun. Others had spread out blankets and picnics, content to lie back with books and coffees and relax the afternoon away. It's a fabulous place to wander and just breathe.

Several years previously, we'd walked through the Heath on our way to Kenwood House, passing the men's and women's bathing ponds – which are separate. Since watching Imelda Staunton, Celia Imrie, Timothy Spall et al., in *Finding Your Feet* I'd wanted to come back to the ponds. We stood, watching several young women launch themselves into the murky water. It's hard to believe, but people swim here all year round. I thought you must almost have to crack the ice to get in during winter.

"Fancy a dip?" Steve asked, grinning and nodding at the women at the edge of the pond.

"Yuck, no thanks!" I screwed up my nose at him. "It looks so reedy and green. It must be okay though, otherwise people wouldn't swim there. Not my idea of fun but I've heard it's meant to be good for you, physically and psychologically."

On we went to Chalk Farm High Street and up to Primrose Hill. The hunger-inducing aromas from lunchtime cooking, wafting out of the restaurants and street stalls, tempted me to bin our sandwiches, but I stayed strong, and we munched our way through them, sitting atop Primrose Hill in the glorious winter sunshine, with hundreds of other people, and just loving the spectacular, clear views of the city.

A fabulous day out walking and, with the temperatures rising, it wouldn't be too long before we'd be back in the park next door, perched on our bench seat – my happy place.

February Snippet

Birthday tarts. It was high time our French Tarts group met up again so, Izzy (our most proficient French-speaking tart), decided I needed to celebrate my birthday and booked the four of us for lunch at The Kings Head bistro pub in the High Street. At several points in the conversation, my eyes darted about the room, checking that we weren't disturbing other pub guests, as we were getting rather raucous, chatting, having fun, eating fabulous food, sharing a bottle of French rosé and catching up on each other's lives. I so enjoyed these women – every one of us so different from the other.

Walking home afterwards, the sunny yellow daffodils dancing in the breeze and perky purple crocus popping up beside our driveway brought a smile to my face, knowing spring was on our heels and life was good. I couldn't wait for the long summer days to arrive.

The following link will take you directly to photos associated with February. Feel free to comment on any of them.

https://bit.ly/LLA_February-2019

Epilogue

One year had flown passed. I hadn't once felt homesick and had only looked forward. It had been a year full of life, full of joy and full of new experiences. What would the next year hold? There was so much more to see and do.

We'd booked a visit to Arundel Castle in West Sussex, the *Antiques Road Show* was coming to Morden Hall Park, Portugal was waiting for us, a trip back to see friends in France was in the pipeline, a walk around Stonehenge had been arranged and taste sensations in Bologna, Bergamot and Milan would be devoured. The North Coast 500 road trip in the Scottish Highlands with friends, Margo and Tom, would follow.

At 61, life was indeed rich and awash with new adventures. I was thrilled to bits we hadn't stayed in Auckland looking for a suitable job. Instead, we'd dared to dream and live the life we had imagined. We'd had a brilliant year and the coming one was shaping up to be even better.

Message from the Author

Thank you so very much for reading my book and I hope you really enjoyed it. Please would you leave a review on Amazon and/or Goodreads? I would be extremely grateful as these reviews greatly influence potential readers and push books up the ranks.

Photos are linked by month on my Facebook page listed below. You don't need a Facebook account to visit this page or to see the photos. And you don't have to divulge any information or join up.

I'd love to have your comments and am happy to answer any questions so do please get in touch with me through:

Email: annemarierawson@gmail.com
Facebook: www.facebook.com/latelifeadventures
Website: www.annemarierawson.com

If you enjoy reading memoirs, I recommend you pop over to the Facebook group, We Love Memoirs, to chat with readers, other authors and me. They have been incredibly supportive of me, an untrained writer, and it's the friendliest and warmest group of people I've met. If you're thinking of writing your memoir and need help, do get in touch with Victoria Twead, a very successful author and owner of <u>Ant Press</u>, the company that helped me publish my books.

This book, and my other books, *My French Platter* and *My French Platter Replenished*, are available through Amazon or, if you are in New Zealand, through:

Poppies, Howick, Auckland
Linen & Stone, Cambridge
Wardini Books, Havelock North and Napier

Or you can order directly through me. Just get in touch.

Thank you!

RECIPES

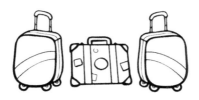

There are only a few recipes, with the first three mentioned in the book. The other two are seasonal favourites. Enjoy.

Pork Wellington

Ingredients
1 kg pork mince (very lean)
1 egg
2 tbsp panko breadcrumbs
1 tbsp dried mixed herbs
½ tsp cracked black pepper
1 tsp salt
2 tbsp seeded mustard (or more to taste)
1 packet of sliced prosciutto
400 gm (14 oz) block savoury puff pastry
1 beaten egg with 1 tsp water for egg wash

Method
Mix together pork mince, egg, breadcrumbs, mixed herbs, pepper and salt. (Much easier to use your hands to squelch it all together.)
Shape into a fat tube, wrap in plastic wrap (or similar) and refrigerate for 30 mins.
Roll out your pastry big enough to wrap about your pork tube.

Remove pork from refrigerator, place on pastry and wrap, creating a one-inch seam.

Seal your seam with egg wash.

Close in each end to totally enclose your pork, sealing the seam again with egg wash.

Turn the whole thing over so that the seam is on the bottom and place on baking paper on suitable oven tray.

Place in the refrigerator for 30 mins or until ready to bake.

Just before placing in hot oven, brush the top and sides of the pastry case with the egg wash.

Cut four air slits across the top only, being careful not to cut the sides of the parcel.

Bake on fan bake at 200 °C/390 °F for 50 mins to ensure pork is cooked and pastry is golden.

Walnut Meringue

Ingredients
5 large egg whites
300 gm (10 oz) castor sugar
180 gm (6 oz) walnuts, crushed
300 ml (½ pint) cream, whipped
icing sugar for dredging

Lemon Curd
¾ cup fresh lemon juice
¾ cup white sugar
½ cup unsalted butter, cubed
3 large eggs
1 tablespoon grated lemon zest

Meringue Method
1. Line two 20 cm (8 in) sandwich tins with silicone paper or draw two 23 cm (9 in) circles on the silicone paper. **Or, if you want to make individual ones, see note below.**

2. Beat egg whites, adding half the sugar as you go and the

remainder folded well in at the end of whisking. Mixture should stand up in peaks.

3. Fold in crushed walnuts with a slotted spoon. Spoon this mixture equally into two tins. Bake at 175 °C/350 °F (fan bake 155 °C/300 °F) for 35–45 minutes, or longer, depending on your oven. Cakes should be crisp on outside. Turn out carefully onto wire tray when done.

4. Fill cake with whipped cream and lemon curd – dust liberally with icing sugar and pass strawberry or raspberry coulis separately.

Curd Method
1. Combine lemon juice, sugar, butter, eggs, and lemon zest in a 2.25-litre (2-quart) saucepan.
2. Cook over medium-low heat, whisking constantly, until mixture thickens and bubbles, about 5–6 minutes.
You can make curd up to one week ahead of use. Cover surface with plastic wrap and store in the refrigerator.

Note: to make individual ones, just draw a circle for how big you want each one and fill the circle accordingly with some meringue mixture. Follow the recipe then, using the back of a dessertspoon, smooth a hollow in the top of each one, then smooth the sides or leave 'rough' if you want. Cook the same as above. Once cool, fill the hollow with your choice of cream, lemon curd and top with whatever fruit you like.

Smoked Salmon, Orange, Beetroot and Feta Entrée

Ingredients
large packet of smoked salmon
three large beetroot
balsamic vinegar
olive oil
½ tsp sugar
two oranges
feta for crumbling
vinaigrette or pomegranate molasses dressing, or a tablespoon
of grated horseradish for serving.

Method
Scrub beetroot clean and place on enough tinfoil to enclose as
a parcel.
Over the beetroot, sprinkle a dash of olive oil and balsamic
vinegar and the sugar.
Close up and seal the tinfoil.
Bake at 200 °C/390 °F for one hour.
Remove from oven and leave to cool in tinfoil.
Peel and segment the oranges, ensuring all pith is removed.

Plate the salmon up around the perimeter of a side plate, grate a portion of beetroot in the centre, adding segments of oranges on top.

Crumble feta over and serve with a sprinkling of vinaigrette or pomegranate molasses dressing or add a tablespoon of horseradish to the plate.

Asparagus Tart

This is a great lunch recipe or a light dinner. I make it often when it's asparagus season. We almost have asparagus for breakfast, lunch and dinner and Steve gets sick of them! I don't.

Ingredients
1 sheet of prepared puff pastry
1 egg, beaten
4 egg yolks
2 bunches of asparagus, with the stalky ends snapped off
200 gm (7 oz) crème fraiche
2 ½ tsp of horseradish or seeded mustard
100 ml (just under half a cup or 3 ½ fl oz) cream
Handful of fresh thyme leaves or chives or parsley
Grated parmesan

Method
Preheat oven to 210 °C.
Lay pastry in a pie tray and brush with egg.
Leave a half inch space from edge of pastry then lay asparagus in a tight row along the base to fit inside the space.

Mix together crème fraiche, egg yolks, choice of herbs, horseradish (or mustard) and cream.

Add salt & pepper to taste.

Pour mixture over the asparagus, top with parmesan and bake for 35 minutes.

Eat while hot with a salad of choice on the side or on its own.

Curried Pork Sausages

We LOVE sausages and we love spice and heat in our food. This recipe is one my mother made when we were kids and now something I make often in the winter. I think there are many variations online and you can add your vegetables to it or have them on the side. These curried sausages are just delicious.

Ingredients
1 kg good quality pork sausages
2 medium onions (or 1 large) sliced
2 ½ cups water
2 tbsp flour
1 tbsp sugar
½ cup water
1 tbsp of each: curry powder (I use hot), Worcestershire sauce, malt vinegar and tomato sauce
Salt & pepper

Method

Grill the sausages, slice and set aside. OR: remove skin from sausage, slice into pieces and gently fry in a little olive oil in a pan.

Once cooked, set aside.

In the same pan use butter or a little olive oil and fry the sliced onions.

Once cooked, add first measure of water.

Mix together the remaining ingredients and add to the pot to thicken.

Add the sausages to heat through.

Serve with creamy mashed potato and the vegetables of your choice.

Printed in Great Britain
by Amazon

40385886R00128